YOU MATTER

Heal ourselves. Heal our children. Heal the World.

YOU MATTER

Heal ourselves. Heal our children. Heal the World.

JOYCE FERN GLASSER, PH.D

To offer comments or ask questions of
the author in mattering style, email:
drjoyceglasser@aol.com

Other than the usual sources for purchasing a book,
you may wish to share with family and friends
these easy ways to order directly:
www.drjoyceglasser.com

Published by: Heart of the Golden Triangle Publishers, Mt. Dora, Florida

Printed in the United States of America

U.S. Library of Congress cataloging publication

With profound gratitude for:

JOYCE ANN MORRIS

An unconditionally loving Energy

SHIRLEY ELLEN ANDERSON

A leader for making a difference

ARNOLD VAN DEN BERG

A man who inspired me to find

the rest of my way to mattering.

Contents

Part 2
Core Healing - From Illness to Wellness

Part 3

Wellness As A Way of Life

In this book, Dr. Glasser provides a public service to those who suffer from "not mattering."

This is the root of all mental illnesses and, to some extent, a cause of discomfort to almost all of us.

When we live thinking that "we don't matter," our minds end up storing a self-image that we are deficient, without us being fully aware of it.

I have experienced how this can lead to depression, anger, diseases, and various addictions.

Dr. Glasser explains the whole process of the writing mechanics of our self-image, which often start in our childhood, where we are easily influenced by our parents and others.

As a result, too many of us end up holding the idea that we will only "matter if" we have good grades, get a good job, earn a lot of money, own fancy houses and cars, etc.

Through more than thirty-five years of practice in working with people with various diseases and addictions, Dr. Glasser helps us understand how our beliefs, both conscious and subconscious, shape the habits and outcomes of our daily lives.

As we read this book, we become aware of how beliefs are formed and reinforced. We come to understand how they direct our actions, and create our reality.

In addition, we realize how these beliefs impact our society by creating inequality, discrimination, and many other self-reinforcing negative behaviors that lead to depression and diseases.

Dr. Glasser opens the possibility of a healthier world, driven by unconditional love — where we can love ourselves as much as our kids and neighbors.

She brilliantly reminds us why we all matter, regardless of what others may say or think. And she provides practical solutions to heal the "core of our being," our identity.

The examples provided in this book are very instructive in that regard. We can feel love radiating through the pages of this book, coming with no "ifs" attached – true, unconditional love.

I hope that you enjoy reading and learning from this book as much as I did and apply its healthy prescriptions to improve your life.

My own experience is that, regardless of your starting point, you can have an exceptional life. It works, and it is a battle that you are sure to win.

Only the extent of your victory may vary. The story of a patient with Parkinson's Disease, who managed to improve her outcome, is especially impressive in that regard.

Please keep in mind that every one of us, by fixing our identities, contributes to a better world (healthier, wiser, happier, more enjoyable). We all have a responsibility in this contribution.

Dr. Glasser has her point: We all truly matter.

Introduction

During the writing of this book about fostering mind-body wellness, a deluge of tragedies occurred. The mental health of many of our young and middle-aged people was already severely on the decline. As a psychotherapeutic professional, I *seek the truth as to what one believes as the path to cure.* The truth in our Country and much of the world is we suffer from the "golden calf syndrome." Here, over time, our Constitution got flipped from the primacy of people mattering to the supremacy of Corporations. That is a key source of our un-wellness.

Majorly erupting in our Country at the time I started writing was depression, anxiety, drug abuse and suicide. As a mental health professional, I kept digging for what word or words could peg the source for this mind-body illness growing so out-of-control. For those so effected, failure seemed their future, and, success out of reach. Simply, the 'bar' was getting too high.

Drilling down, narrowing it down still farther, what was the destructive messaging people at all socio-economic levels were increasingly receiving? What killer messaging was causing this terrible trend of meaninglessness, suffering and death?

I paused. I reflected. I witnessed. I focused. And finally, one core concept became clear as key to this mental illness pandemic and was born out so horrifically as recently as January 6, 2021. Implicitly and explicitly scripted, people believe they are not good enough to matter, or not matter unless they were the richest or the most powerful.

And, in this latest tragedy, hordes were led to believe their votes didn't matter. To them, *implicitly* that meant they didn't matter. The pain evoked aided in generating violent follower-ship for that pain's relief.

Systematically, people's minds were being brain washed to enslave, and earlier to acquiesce to a work ethic so inhuman as to become overworked while being paid less and less. More and more people were made to feel they didn't matter or only mattered if they are rich, beautiful, smart, handsome, get into the 'right' schools, belong to the right political party, get married and have children, are straight, white, male, and not care too much about the science of truth that was telling us our world was dying. So now, the World itself wasn't mattering too.

Our survival was and is unquestioningly at stake. Stressed people were and are internalizing and suffering mentally and physically as a fear based result of not mattering and now many more even to themselves.

The Corona Virus mismanagement amplified our not mattering status. Ever since, we are experiencing an existential crisis magnified to the max generating an exponential amount of anti-human not mattering. While all lives are at stake, mostly the poorer ones, as usual, are the ones most victimized.

Huge numbers of lives are being treated like they don't matter and have been dying in the thousands. Until we live in a society where You Matter, that the quality of the life of each and <u>every</u> one of you matters <u>equally</u>, until we reverse course and propel <u>all</u> of ourselves forward as ethically mattering human beings, poverty, ignorance, fear, depression, suffering and death will continue to ravage us.

Since the fear of Communism and becoming a world power pervaded our psyches, more and more types of people were mattering less and less. Money, Corporate power, industrial sized farming, and in a sense Rand type of entitlement plus a falsely founded sense of supremacy came to matter more than you, I or the rioters themselves. Our saving grace "love" was disappearing.

For decades, tabloid news outlets have aided and abetted our not mattering. When truth is not told and/or misleading prevails a form of mind control for a huge profit and consequent power enslaves and degrades reality. 'Move over China'!

With such mind control, our mental wellness is on the line. Our lives and those of others like the farmers in India who want to matter too are on the line as are the lives of immigrants. And yes, utilizing 'due process', we can make sure not to overload our 'raft' but at the same time *cruelty must not prevail*. Condoning cruelty is mental illness personified.

To matter equally <u>requires</u> allowing our natural inclination toward utilizing kindness to flourish. Evolving as humans, we were enhanced with this kindness tool, this kindness inclination. We have seen the practicality of transitioning from raw, snarling animal power to survive, replaced with kindness. Imagine the number of ways the quality of wholesome connectivity enriches us. Normal fears of winding up alone recede. Feelings of comfort replace such fear based ones. Take a moment, think about how good kindliness actually does *feel*, how safe, how healthy, how wonderful it is to give <u>and</u> to receive, how heartening, how calming to bear witness to its being given and received.

This past year, it has been beautiful to observe people of all ages helping each other, offering creative, caring charitable solutions, holding the lives of neighbors as sacred by quarantining and wearing masks and/or keeping their distance during this time of dangerous pandemics. Plural? I count about nine of them. So, yes more than one pandemic. There is more than just the deadly Covid and its variants we are witnessing. Another, is people not mattering to themselves and thus acting with indifference and worse violence and cruelty toward others.

The 65 year old retired Naval man, a leader of the January 6, 2021 insurrectionists, talked about "mattering". I wish I had his exact words. My guess is, the guy was looking for and found a cause that would make him feel like he did with his shipmates in common cause.

Mattering equally and with kindness is humanity's antidote to whatever the type of virus. Now, multiply the marvelous ways kindness can be evidenced with self and neighbors. As we do that, we raise the potential for what I refer to as brain-body wellness to exponential levels. That could happen. We are at that unique, pivotal moment in the history of humankind. Salvation's choice is at hand: wellness **or** illness? *Illness foments war and poverty.* Wellness leads to peace and prosperity.

What would the result be to choosing wellness via mattering? What would you witness out over time? Literally, illness, pain and suffering in all its forms would begin to subside and then much of it even disappearing.

Through and through wellness cannot exist without a kindness recipe. So, a Glossary of Wellness Beliefs as *truth* enhancing values to live by are provided after Chapter 12. *Good health, love and peace can only reign as a result of wellness commitment and the needed wellnesses' skills taught.*

Think about it. What we are really talking about out over time is illness prevention. Cure is mostly about *fixing* our mistakes. Prevention is about lessening the need for cures , eliminating their expenses and most of all reducing huge amounts of pain and suffering from happening in the first place.

Preventing mental and physical illness is the ultimate goal of this book. The knowledge to do that is here. With that knowledge, we can not only prevent much illness both of mind and body but create an environment where over the coming decades, we are fostering a humane evolution revolution by fully integrating into one's being an ease with wellness actualization. Loving, purposed living potential can indeed become enhanced. My effort here is to help people realize, that mattering kindly, that mattering equally is not just about justice. What is majorly at stake is the huge potential for minimizing pain and suffering for everyone even the white, male, supremacists so afraid of being found out for the enormity of their own perceived inadequacies. I know. I have worked with many of them.

When you commit to mattering with gentleness and kindness for self and others that's the path to brain-body wellness victory. You become a part of the solution to ridding our world of suffering and destruction. Advances in "....ending mental illness" (Daniel Amen, MD) are heartening. I know how elated I have felt either improving or curing mental and physical illnesses when conducting what my clients call Core Healing.

Conducting Core Healing has taught me that what seemed so complicated is actually rather simple. Living in our bodies as the precious Sanctuaries that they are, allows not just mental wellness but substantial reduction of psychogenic illness including many types of cancer and heart disease. You can't enjoy this gift if you don't matter but only if you do.

Core Healing as explained in this book is fascinating. It is a truth seeking, belief remedying journey into the consciously unknown but available truths with which to resolve problems whether of mind or body. I have years worth of records to document my findings from such journeys.

Core Healing can most easily be achieved when in a heightened awareness state that either a meditative or hypnotic induction can access. When a person's sense of mattering is at unhealthy levels that person's wellness and the lives they touch, all are threatened. I want your lives saved by the fact that you matter, have equal worth and enjoy actualizing kindness with self and others. That's true heroic conduct.

Either not mattering or seeing you and yours as all that matter are death sentences for self and others. Subconsciously, you may not even realize that you were raised in such a way as to conclude you don't matter or that only you and yours matter. I see you as pained souls who are among the walking dead. You are the grim reapers. You're the terrorists, you're the murderers, you're the dictators, you're the power hungry, you're the rape apes, you're the supremacists. If we follow you, at least in part, *we are you*. The opportunity for a life of loving mattering diminishes, even ceases. Your children usually die inside learning how not to healthfully matter by your example.

Thus, the fact is that the real heroes of our future are those who do their best to be among the meek, the gentle and the kind. The real heroes are those who repair and/or improve themselves as suggested here. I call this: "self re-parenting". What needs re-parenting about self allows you to better parent your children both wisely and well. There's no shame in the realization that there is no such thing as a perfect parent. The only shame is not improving ourselves. The latter as shame is the escape from the Fourth R: responsibility.

United, we can create Villages of wholesome cultures based upon admirable current and past history that emphasizes and praises our progress as humane beings. With truth and a keen sense of equality and kindliness, neighbors living comfortably integrated, wholesomeness oriented lives exemplifying wellness is the greatest gift we can give our children. And, because You Matter, this book was birthed to help you live and breathe that truth.

And so I ask.......

Is peace on Earth going to begin with you?

I'm 'all in' to continue improving myself

for such purpose.

Join me?

Dr. Joyce Glasser

The purpose of this book is to demonstrate that every individual has the potential to be a happy and healthy person who is able to make positive contributions not only in their own life but also in the lives of their families, their friends, their community and the world. Yet so many people fall short of this potential.

Why is that? If you've ever wondered why you were not able to achieve your fullest and most meaningful potential, you will not only find the answers in this book, but you will also find the solutions!

Drawing upon thirty-five years of professional experience working with people who have had a wide variety of problems, Dr. Glasser developed a methodology that helped them achieve their goals in a short period of time. In her book, "You Matter", Dr. Glasser points to the origin of how one's problems started. During our childhood, most of us were not aware that our emotional problems were most likely created by our parents, relatives, and friends. We simply accepted their voices as truths even though many of their comments were not the truth at all! Nevertheless, whatever was told to us affected our personal beliefs and created feelings, behaviors, and attitudes. Ultimately, this led to the outcome of our lives.

Through the practice of hypnosis, as a mental health professional, Dr. Glasser treated more than one thousand people and drew her conclusions upon their case histories. Within this book, she shares many reasons for peoples' problems as well as providing "real-life" examples of how their problems came about and she offers you, the reader, understandable solutions. By following the principles Dr. Glasser brings to your attention, you will find it easier to achieve your goals and you will find yourself "living a life that truly matters!"

Although the focus of emotional and behavioral problem resolutions is on every therapist's agenda, many therapists are not able to reach their client's goals since most people do not even remember the time in their life when their problems started! Through hypnosis, Dr. Glasser has been able to walk her clients back-in-time and was able to discover the true causes that created some of their limiting or destructive belief(s) and replace them with truthful positive ones.

I personally experienced an incident in my own life that limited my ability to achieve something I consciously wanted. Even though I had five years of therapy dealing with problems that I experienced as a holocaust survivor, I did not realize that my mother programmed my mind not to have children. The reason my mother put those negative thoughts into my mind was to spare me the agonizing pain that she experienced each day while she was in the concentration camp of Auschwitz. Although my brother and I were hidden at the time, she worried endlessly whether or not we would be discovered and survive that terrible war.

As a child, I was not aware of the power of her words that were strongly imprinted upon my subconscious mind. On a conscious level, as I grew to adulthood, I wanted to have children. When I realized that I was still not able to achieve this blessing, I went back to the psychiatrist who treated me previously. At this time in his practice, he included the use of hypnosis. After three sessions of hypnosis, he found the cause of my problem and was able to solve it. Within a month of the three hypnotic sessions, my wife became pregnant!

By following the very informative and loving advice that Dr. Glasser offers in her book, you will be able to manage and overcome your personal problems and plant positive seeds by which you will be able to better govern your life. Once you understand the causes of your problems, it will be much easier for you to correct them. Achieving your goals opens a new horizon in which you will find that you're living a much better life and, indeed, a healthier life! This is the life you have been desiring and the life you truly deserve! By accomplishing this, Dr. Glasser will have realized her dream of taking all the knowledge and experience that she gained over a life-time to show people that they are important and that their life is a "Life that Matters"!

In summary, within this book, you will be able to find the help you have been searching for... the help that will systematically change your beliefs of the past to "success-oriented beliefs" going forward. Once you have accomplished this, you will find ways to inspire your family, friends, co-workers, and your community to believe in positive ways that can change their lives too! This first step in changing your world.

Part 1
MATTERING - HUMANITY'S ANTIVIRUS

1

Understanding the Urgency of You Mattering

Urgent: Compelling or requiring immediate action or attention; imperative; pressing.

Urgency: If there's urgency to a situation, it's a pressing issue and you have to respond quickly; an earnest and insistent need.

Most, if not all of us, are victims of identity theft. It is of a sort so dangerous it also threatens the Earth's existence. The denial of one's valuable identity allows for subjugating to the point of even working people to death. One's wellness potential is stolen.

Whether in our homes ruled by a tyrannical parent, or by an obnoxious boss, a dictator, an agent of God's unquestioned word, or any other type of supremacist, all rob us of our truth in service to their imperialism. They are the thieves. They steal our wellness right along with the essentialness of our mattering.

Mattering has been stolen from the multitudes throughout history. It's even worse now. Dark despair is settling over us.

Despairing thoughts can be communicated in some of the following ways:

"I don't feel relevant."

"I feel so abandoned and alone."

"I feel so stressed."

"Through the decades nothing ever changes."

Through the use of hypno-analytics, my clients taught me that their relevant foundational experiences that lead to such ideas or identities are spoken of differently. The language used above often means nothing therapeutically. Those concepts are adult concepts.

Core healing, a hypno-therapeutic process, reinforces the knowledge that about 80 percent of our foundational identities are formed by age six and, therefore, those identities are in the language of a child. A key, universal and ever so critical one is "well, I guess I just don't matter."

Until a person at core believes they matter, they can quickly shrivel and die. Suicide looms as a last resort for those lacking the basic understanding that they matter, that they have value.

Those who fundamentally feel they don't matter are also plagued with the companion belief: "I'm not good enough." This is then compounded with beliefs that other people are either smarter, prettier, richer, stronger, faster, thinner, etc. Not believing oneself to be good enough in whatever ways generally entrenches the feelings of not mattering.

If we want to create wellness in all of our children, one way is to develop a keen sense of their own unique strengths. From the very beginning of their development observe them. Look for their strengths. Whenever you notice one — including something like their ease with getting over being sick or how well they are doing with focusing on a task or what interesting structures they create with their Legos — let them know, but without exaggeration, with words that you can only speak with absolute conviction. Supporting and providing opportunities for their skill development in the arenas of their strengths and interests shape their identities for the better.

Enhancing those strengths they particularly enjoy contributes to their sense of mattering. It helps develop positive self-concepts and beliefs based on that authentic experience with themselves. In other words, these positive and *true* experiences create healthy mind-body imprints, positive identities for their computer-like brain to implement as they grow up.

Here's an example of how we can use words to reinforce ourselves and those around us. We can use language such as, "Each one of us has talents that are fun to grow. " Set the example. Then, with such emphasis, a sense of equality and the competence of others will allow children to thrive and appreciate rather than fear "the other" as they move forward to adulthood.

Inequality is the enemy of mattering. Dominance, supremacy, dictatorships, dons, the leaders of criminal empires — those powers with smoke and mirrors — are fiddling with your future while our world burns and riots. They have bunkers. Have they built them for the rest of us? No! So, don't be fooled by them. You matter.

Homogeneous Switzerland bases its society and commerce on equality. While it is still a capitalistic nation, it creates balance by offering citizens a way to live with relative equality — no one being more important than anyone else. They strive toward equality of opportunity. The middle class is alive and well, as is a quality of life for all citizens. Yet, they do so without losing their capability for healthy, wholesome competition within the world's marketplace. Finland, by the way, is another fine example of "you matter" capitalism. When US citizenship in and of itself is seen as the conveyor of homogeneity, "you matter" capitalism can happen here.

In those parts of the world where the male demands dynastic supremacy, which means that everyone else, not just women, matter less, poverty wages generally prevail. That type of inequality causes a kind of systemic 'unwellness' that bleeds into every aspect of society. It is unwholesomely painful to make others feel they don't matter *unless* they are: the strongest, richest, most well-connected, most powerful, most famous, the 'right' ethnicity or religion, the 'winningest,' etc. More than that, such contemptible positioning of humankind is igniting dangerous outcomes. Wars, rioting and terrorism are growing ever more deadly. Our children, our neighbors, our young people, our middle-aged unemployed men, and our sexually abused and sex-enslaved youngsters, are prey to the "you only matter if" or "only I matter" epidemic.

People are suffering. In so many ways, one group or another, as well as employees, is being added to the "not mattering" list, either explicitly or implicitly. People are being enslaved not necessarily with chains but by fostering ignorance through the degradation of our public schools and also a ridiculously unhealthy work demand that saps the joy out of life. Pain results. Stress grows. Bodies' immune systems decline. Illness sets in. Well-being becomes minimized. Consequently, people become dependent on substances like prescription and nonprescription drugs, alcohol, vaping, and other toxic distractions. Ultimately, those individuals become dependent on nurses, doctors, parents, to deal with their dependencies, their suicidal ideation. We are reaching crisis levels of this kind of epidemic. It's becoming more and more urgent as struggling individuals increasingly face isolation, loss and unemployment.

On the other hand, when individuals truly believe at core that they matter, it's easier to be respectful of self and others. That results in healthier lifestyles and the kind of cooperation that is required to be well both mentally and physically. In a sense, mental and physical wellness are one and the same. When people actually believe they matter, it is easier to be decent and kind with themselves.

Another important benefit of mattering is that we are less prone to the upper ranges of anger. Anger manifests itself in the following ways:
• Punitive, by punishing others and very much so ourselves.
• Vindictive, by achieving satisfaction from causing others and ourselves pain.
• Guilt-ridden, not allowing for self-forgiveness, and creating anger often turned inward and/or outward.
• Raging, by showing our anger in loud bursts that bump up against or come near to violence.
• Violence, by physically hurting others the way we feel we have been hurt.
• And at its worst, murderous. We take another person's life and often end by taking our own.

If, when raised with a personal sense of mattering unconditionally or if later as adults, we come to believe at core that we matter, our thinking about, our judgment regarding the importance of our own wellness improves. After all, we now have worth and the freedom to make a constructive, loving difference each in our own way.

Our behavior becomes more self-care oriented. Consequently, individuals who believe they matter are more able to be receptive to the realization of self-punitive conduct. They are freer to rid themselves from the damage resulting from their own punishment fitting the crime. As an issue, it can be more rationally addressed, lessened and ideally eliminated.

Importantly, there is greater receptivity to the idea that if I matter, you matter, too. Compassion can grow and vendetta's teachings can be replaced with empathetic comprehension. We can acknowledge our own thoughtless behavior and theirs. Forgiving our mistakes, forgiving theirs, become available as a remedy to lessening pain, suffering, and the fears that ignite the worst in learned human behavior.

When that ragingly painful "sore spot" of not mattering is gone, our potential for violence diminishes. But sadly, in the United States, more than seven people per hour die a violent death. More than 19,500 people were victims of homicide and more than 47,000 people died by suicide in 2017 alone. If that doesn't scream mattering's "urgency," what does? Regrettably, deafeningly, there is an answer to that question. The indifference of far too many to the human toll due to the laissez-faire approach to the coronavirus and racism screams ever louder.

All of us "mattering" equally is about life and death. It's critical to our future. I call mattering humanity's antivirus. Knowing we matter makes us more eager to learn from tragedies. We have a better sense of perspective and deeper need for understanding our world. You've heard the old expression, "ignorance is bliss." People who feel that they don't matter prefer to be ignorant, not because they're less intelligent or in some way inferior, but because ignorance can be a form of numbing oneself. Perhaps the expression should be, "ignorance is an excuse." It certainly is an escape from responsibility.

Mattering strengthens us at the cellular level, and I have a supposition that mattering is supportive of longevity. Mattering nurtures having a sense of purpose, "making a difference" and therefore gives us a reason to live longer. *Mattering heals us from the inside out.* I admit that my theory of longevity needs to be researched, but this belief is founded in a lifetime of my own and my clients' experiences, having worked more than thirty-five years in the mental health field.

The person who, at core, knows they matter can enjoy the true fun of sharing. They can do so wholeheartedly. Sharing knowledge, wealth, good fortune, even a simple and healthy recipe, is more fun when it's a matter of "sharing is caring," as Madeleine Sherak in 2018 said in a delightful children's book she wrote.

Not sharing, not caring can be called negatively selfish. That conduct is more likely from those who believe only they matter. On the other hand, one who believes: "I don't matter *unless* I am being good to my neighbor" — that person is more prone to sharing and caring and less prone to being negatively selfish toward others.

Not mattering as in becoming negatively selfish, leads to: Why should you matter if I don't? Why should I give you my lecture notes just because you missed the class? Fail, it's what you deserve. Why should I donate to the poor? They should have worked harder. Their lot is not my problem. Others not mattering leads to cruelty, suffering and death for the doer and the receiver.

The Dalai Lama said we are all selfish. Selfishness can be both of the good kind or of the negative. The ideal position is being wholesomely selfish. Some choices must be weighted toward ourselves. We can't help anyone if we ourselves are out of balance or if we are unwell financially, physically, or mentally. It's the airplane concept of putting your air mask on first before your child's or even anyone else's.

We are fundamentally hardwired to be good and to be cooperative. It's fun to matter and be helpful. We learn the skills of being that much more quickly when we're taught we matter. The Earth is dying because too many people do not matter and, by extension, the Earth doesn't matter either. Mattering funnels down to the issue of survival.

Try to imagine what it would be truly like if you don't matter. As mentioned earlier, there is cause and effect. If you don't matter you quite literally would "shrivel and die." The Earth is experiencing that trickle-down effect and it's dying. It's not a matter of if, it's a matter of how soon.

Consider universal common cause versus insular cause: All of us mattering or only myself and my cohorts mattering.

Universal Common Cause

Taking care of the Earth is a universal common cause. There are so many sub efforts but not one that orchestrates, nor unites all efficiently. Steel reserve, clarity of vision, experience, the ability to delegate and harness brilliance would be qualifications for the leadership required. That wisest, most skilled of leaders would have the primary qualification of leading from the heart with passion and dedication.

If our nurturing birthing source plus our mother Earth sustenance source, if they don't matter, we don't survive. Eventually, mountains of money will be burnt to a crisp.

Uniting all nurturing causes for climate survival makes sense. It can be cost effective and focused under one roof of vision and mission statements.

A company in Boca Raton, Florida, called 4Ocean uses money from sales of its products to remove trash from the ocean. Buy a bracelet made from recycled materials, and for each bracelet sold, 4Ocean will remove a pound of trash from the ocean and coastlines.

The common cause leadership makes sure to assess the value of that program. If conceptually solid, it disseminates that knowledge around the coastlines of the world.

With Bombas Socks, you buy a pair and they donate a pair to a person experiencing homelessness. Our homelessness issue is actually a universal common cause that when we have some degree of mattering ourselves, we can be more active in such empathetic service to others. Every worthy program gets the support of the common cause resources.

Insular Cause

An insular cause follows only the ideas and doctrines of the group's leaders. In many churches, we learn that vengeance by God awaits sinners and the fear of God is good. Members are taught what to think and what matters. There is no creativity, no adventuring. This thinking narrows the possible; in fact, it shuts alternative beliefs down. How much better would we live in awe of God instead of in fear? The Hebrew word for "awe" can be translated either as "fear" or as "awe." Why was "fear" acceptable to include in both Testaments?

Insular causes tend to center around power and money. Fear-based people are easier to manipulate. Poorly informed people are easier to control. To foster insular causes, broad-based, scientific or logic-based knowledge and learning are not embraced.

Education is key to mattering so you can relate meaningfully to others. Formal education enlightens us and helps prepare us in many ways, but knowledge also awaits us in many places. Learning and its companion of social skills development are the foundation of relationships.

I love the word "loam." It refers to fertile soil. The seed of eternal life planted in the loam of loving kindness is about lovability and quality mattering. In other words, in order to love, another must matter. When we are fully nurtured in such loam, we thrive and that becomes transmittable. We transmit "mattering," and thus the warm-hearted loam of each life and of our Earth is enhanced.

Not mattering creates force and aggression. Have you noticed those most often enshrined as heroes are usually aggressive? Even in *Star Wars* the expression was, "Let the Force be with you." I would love to see those words replaced with the words, "May eternal kindness forever connect us." Another way to say it is: Let the eternal loving energy be within us to s h a r e— not the force that 'might makes right'. May loving energy be our connection.

If You Don't Matter, What Does?

Sooner or later, and quite literally, if you do not matter, you die. Life has no meaning, no need for purposeful existence. Emptiness and worthlessness take over, and such feelings are very painful. It is my belief that the absence of mattering is the root of all mental illness and many people are led to believe that they don't matter from a very early age. That belief does not go away without "seeing" the truth of its presence. When that epiphany occurs, that aha! moment, then freedom to healthfully matter follows.

Consider the makeup of the terrorist. They are set up to kill, to destroy lives. Do you think such a person believes they matter? Well, at least in their death, they hope they do. And, in that moment they have power over their fear. They are finally seen. But then they are gone. And, if not by saving the last bullet for themselves, then suicide by cop.

Terrorists have a cause and are taught to die rather than live for it. Such stupid heroism: to be blinded from seeing your own worth and that of others, others than your own kind.

Not mattering begins early. Feelings of not mattering generally start with parental absence or perceived sibling preference. One's survival as an infant and for several years later depends on attention. When wholesome, adequate attention is not available, the self as not mattering sets in. Not mattering is grown in the dirt of perceived abandonment. Later, the belief that you only matter "if" — often meaning by being perfect — is a part of the reinforcement of that sense of personal worthlessness.

"If my child is perfect, that makes me a perfect parent. If they are less than perfect, I am a less than perfect parent."

So, in order to belong, in order to matter, in order to feel worthwhile — when we don't matter — what does?

- Fancy cars
- A big house
- Expensive jewelry

Those are a means to an end. They are a way to demonstrate mattering and being worthy of belonging. They are means with which to dampen a corollary fear of winding up alone. We show our children that having possessions is what matters. If their grades are less than perfect or if they don't excel at something that will lead to getting into the right school/job/career, they won't have the money to be able to get all those tickets of admission, of acceptance. They will fail at demonstrating to others worthiness of belonging, which is akin to issues of survival. It has an odor of "do or die."

When a child feels the pain that he or she only matters *if* . . . a quest for numbness ensues. It's better to be numb than to feel the pain of not mattering much or even at all. Better to be numb than face the idea that you are failing at being good enough. Cruelty, by the way, is another form of numbing. It's pain transference. Bullies are cruel to others so they're not alone in their misery. It's pain sharing. In that sense, misery truly does love company. Parents are often cruel to their children and siblings cruel to one another. Parents may unwittingly contribute to the s u r v i v a l, a t t e n t i o n g e t t i n g competition between siblings, which in turn sets up the inequality that leads to not mattering.

Pain-sharing and numbing take other forms, too. Cutting is a way to self-hypnotically numb oneself. Cutting can also be used to create attention getting physical pain to oneself to distract from the mental anguish felt. Even biting nails to the quick serves such purposes that also include the escape from the pain anxiety creates.

As one continues to actualize the pain accumulating belief that "I don't matter", or "I only matter if", the greater the fear and the nearness of death grow. Faulty afterlife teachings c a n become a scary, pain inducing issue regar ding am I 'deserving' of heaven or hell or just nothingness? The latter two induce further fear generative of pain.

So, the sooner you are dead, then the sooner you get to escape but only the pain of this life. Fear of afterlife may postpone suicide.

Homicide can be a by product of numbing the pain of not mattering and feeling uncared about. And, where caring and empathy isn't cultivated, indifference is fostered and others will die.

There are those who matter not to themselves but survive because they believe they matter to their pet, their children or some cause. When the cause is accomplished, then how does one deal with the pain of not mattering anymore?

Many men are led to believe they only matter if they make lots of money, are good-looking, are athletic or have large penises. Often, women are taught they only matter if they are pretty, thin, big-breasted, sexy yet virginal, sweet, and subservient. Imagine why men are so obsessed about a woman's size.

In addition, when we believe we don't matter, what difference does decency make? "You're not going to love me anyway." "Why should I be nice?   There's no percentage benefit to me in it." So, what matters? You Matter. It's the antidote to not mattering's demeaning existence.

Drugs, Guns, Despair, Suicide, Insanity

Drugs are being used for pain management in previously unheard of numbers, but the pain is not merely physical. That's the surface. Pain is emotional. Drugs numb the feelings of despair.

Guns have created a big debate in America. The fear that the government will take the guns away is a point of contention. Why are there so many guns in America? Guns feed paranoia. They are an antidote for inadequacy. The thinking goes, if I have a gun, I can best the "bad guys."

Guns are a form of power for people who feel powerless. And, the revolution that those armed with the likes of AK 47s are preparing for is an escape from not mattering by getting killed and taking revenge on their imagined perpetrators in the process all the while being delusional in dying for such a cause.

Despair is rampant. People are experiencing feelings of being powerless, worthless. We are working longer and harder for less return. We are told we should be happy but to be happy we need to have possessions, money, position, the love of a partner, or children. When those things fall short more readily, we sink into despair.

This state of despair is not just an economic issue. It is about horrific injustice growing into epic proportions. Our democracy is being ripped to shreds, our Earth as home is being trashed by indifferent corporate interests. Racial discrimination is getting worse, corruption is rampant, how then can your wellness needs, your mattering as wellness necessity be front burnered? The pain of it all is deepening.

Suicide is one escape from the pain. It is the most drastic and final escape. The suicide rate among young people has underscored the ultimate feeling of not mattering, and its companion feelings of not being good enough, along with feeling powerless. The Centers for Disease Control and Prevention show 48,344 people died by suicide in 2018, up from 47,173 the year before. While the increase was small, just two-tenths of a percent, the rise in deaths over time has been steady. Since 1999, the suicide rate has climbed 35 percent. The rate at which young Americans took their own lives reached new highs in 2018, driven by a sharp rise in suicides among older teenage boys. In that year alone, suicide claimed the lives of 5,016 males and 1,225 females between the ages of fifteen and twenty-four in the United States.

Insanity is a way to take a vacation from pain. How many times have you heard someone say, "You're driving me crazy. I can't handle it anymore!"? The *it* in that sentence is the pain. People feel overwhelmed by the demands of current-day survival. So, they check out and wind up in a mental institution or they commit a violent crime based on their anger and wind up in prison. Either way, they go to a place where they will be watched over.

Whatever crazy means to you is how you act. Crazy can just mean shutting out the world to escape the no-longer-manageable self-responsibility. Crazy is a word most often used to explain behavior not understood as to what the actual generative beliefs are .

When you have money, you can at least attempt to find temporary relief from the pain. You can go on vacation, buy a new sports car, get pampered at a spa.

But what if you're poor? What do you do for release? Sometimes you choose extreme actions, drinking and driving, fighting with your significant others, raging at someone on the road. Some of those actions can result in problems with the law, put you on the road to insanity and/or cause your death and the death of another.

How Our Actions Affect Others and the World

If I don't matter and I treat you like you don't matter, how will we treat the world?

If I'm your mother and subconsciously I don't matter, I will pass on to you that you don't matter. I will express that in my words and actions.

"Don't interrupt me — can't you see I'm busy?"

"No, you can't have a cookie. You're getting fat and I can't afford new clothes for you."

Parents are infecting their children with messages that are both unhealthy explicitly (fat) and implicitly (unworthy of love and attention). So, ask yourself, how do these messages make you or anyone else feel? "You're not good enough!" "You can do better." It's never good enough. "You're unlovable as you are." "I have no time for you." These types of messages to one's children develop them with the belief they will only be good enough maybe or if.

When you fawn over someone else's child whom you perceive to be better at something than your own children, you send your children the message they aren't equal — they don't matter as much. Comparing your child's accomplishments to those of other children sets up the endless need to be "as good as." "Robert . . . did you notice that Johnny played his piece in the recital perfectly? You, on the other hand, made three mistakes. Robert, you need to practice more."

By saying something like this, you are really saying that you're not a good enough parent. You didn't make your child practice enough and you're embarrassed by their imperfection. Instead of celebrating all the notes the child got right, the parent focuses on the few mistakes. How can a child feel they matter when that's the case? How often do parents make this kind of mistake and why? Mostly, because parents make the mistake of having to be the perfect parent. Therefore, how must their children perform? Perfectly.

Multimedia and technology can also support not mattering. We are focused on our phones, social media, texting without the emotion that we express when we speak in person or even on a phone call. When we communicate through many types of technology, we can lose our human connection. Innovatively, during this pandemic, technology is adjusting to bring people in proximity at least visually, auditorily and as families, neighbors, coworkers, etc.

During this pandemic I am witnessing a paradox. There is a decrease in distancing while distancing. Not mattering to each other is declining. Regrettably, however, political leadership that engages crony capitalism still conveys the position that you only matter based on to whom and in what ways you show your "loyalty." The power brokers require ever more capital in order to dominate. We in the middle class, the poor, the racially different and the "disloyal" matter less while those power brokers matter in dollars and cents at catastrophic expense to us.

Black and Hispanic populations are increasing in numbers. By the year 2030, minorities will outnumber the white population. There is a fear of retribution. What will those minorities do when they are in the majority? Will they retaliate against the white population, particularly white males, that held them down for so long?

In Israel, the Orthodox Jewish segment wants to be the ruling population. This is also part and parcel of white male supremacy and has much to do with the leadership of its current Prime Minister. Originally, Israel was intended to be welcoming and embracing of all Jews, not just the ultra-Orthodox.

I believe it's time to shift, to swerve. In the Renaissance period, European history marked the transition from the Middle Ages to Modernity. Around the fourteenth century, they began to turn away from barbarism and launched into a period where truth, art, and beauty were the focus. It was a time of rebirth.

Now, our swerve to salvation must be toward mattering. If we embrace each and every child as mattering from the beginning of their existence, when we exemplify for our children that they matter equally, we can expand into the beauty of "loving kindness" sharing. Witnessing the quantity of such lovely, heroic, creative acts of caring has thrilled so many of us to witness as neighbors — regardless of neighborhood — coming together during this tragic time.

This is a time, this is our fateful, sacred moment in time to keep the beauty of this loving kindness alive and growing. Keep in mind as you move forward that there are four states of mattering:

1. I matter (equally and kindly).
2. I don't matter "unless."
3. I don't matter at all.
4. Only I and mine matter.

Once we begin to invest ourselves in the inherent sense that, "I matter *and you* matter," we begin the swerve toward a healthy, wiser, happier, more enjoyable, and lovable life. It holds the promise of a rebirth into a life that can shift our society into salvation and into human nature at her best.

❄

An FYI

For some useful tips on fostering wholesome mattering, there is a new book out copyrighted a couple of months after mine that is also entitled You Matter. It is by Matthew Emerzian.

Do consider using the compatible activities offered in his book.

```
┌─────────────────────────────────┐
│               2                 │
│                                 │
│   Awareness is Half the Battle  │
└─────────────────────────────────┘
```

You've heard the expression that knowing is half the battle. For example, when someone comes to the realization that they are ill, be it physically or mentally, it is then that they can begin to address the problems. But only if they want to take that step and only if their mind allows for it.

What if we become aware, or we already are aware, that we have a problem and yet, we ignore it? What if we decide to do nothing about it or go into denial?

• I don't have cancer or a viral disease. I'm fine.

But the test came back and said you do.

• I'm not stressed.

But your chest is tight, and you can't sleep at night.

• I'm mostly happy; I'm not really depressed.

But you can't get out of bed in the morning and you hate your job.

Awareness is half the battle. So, what's the rest of the battle?

Our Amoral Mind: How Our Beliefs Shape Us

Over time, the human brain creates a neural, governing network of thousands of self concepts and beliefs. There are good beliefs and there are bad ones — meaning that, when implemented, they can cause a person more or less joy, or more or less grief.

Beliefs are implemented based on how they were defined at the time made. A child may come to believe he or she is bad because they don't listen to what they are told to do. Another child also comes to believe he or she is bad because of making mistakes.

Without any sense of right or wrong (amorally), each child's mind-body, will make them act out their definition in response to any stimulus that calls for either of them to be "bad" according to each one's definition. So, how does the child who '*doesn't do what they are told*' a c t when their teacher in school tells that child to sit straight? Might that child react by slouching even more? Yes.

As one's beliefs become imprinted, they are perceived in these three ways:

• True
• The way the world is
• The way he/she is

For example, consider the following belief: "I don't matter as a boy; it's better to be a girl." That's what I call a reactive decision. Most such reactive decisions are made so young, they are not consciously remembered, just enacted. So, whatever being "like a girl" means to that boy determines his behavior, his ethos.

Most of a person's beliefs are not consciously known to that person and therefore are not consciously orchestrated, but rather they exist subconsciously. Quite simply, a stimulus appears through one or more of a human beings' senses and is transmitted to the brain for the "appropriate" reaction, i.e., what the relevant belief(s) dictate.

The person reacts to the stimulus regardless of whether we'd call the response itself appropriate. After several similar reactions, that boy might grow up drawing the conscious conclusion "gee, I talk like a girl."Again, notice the word "appropriate." It's highlighted to open the door further to the idea of amoral mind functioning, meaning the mind does not evaluate a belief that is self or otherwise programmed. The brain reacts based upon the relevant belief(s) according to the stimulus. That's because the reaction,"talking like a girl" is based on the belief held. It is not a reaction the doer himself might consciously judge as a good idea.

Here's an example of how consciously known beliefs can be supported by a consciously unknown belief like "I'm sort of an *outcast."* The example is a decision to vape.

Consciously known beliefs:

Having friends at my new school is important; I want to be accepted and included, and I'm afraid I won't be. It seems like everyone vapes.

But . . . I saw someone on TV who was hospitalized for vaping.

Yes, but . . . they were older, so vaping won't hurt me now. I'm young.

Unhealthy beliefs, those both consciously and not consciously known overrode good judgment, the thought that "maybe I shouldn't." In this example, the negative belief "I'm an outcast" prevailed because it generated the over-riding of good judgment. The belief won, not the thoughts, not the good judgment. And people wonder: why do I do what I know is bad for me? Negative self concepts and beliefs most only subconsciously known produce negative outcomes.

When observing this unhealthy and dangerous — and to some unfathomable — behavior, one reaction could be "oh, she thinks she's immortal." Not all young people vape. So, what's the truth — since they, too, likely have ignorance as to their mortality? The truth has to do whether or not the youth is governed by healthy or unhealthy beliefs relevant to the act of vaping.

Information provided on television or the Internet can seek to inform or scare one into quitting. It strives to push that audience away from harmful activity such as smoking. And, yet, those infomercials will only work for those minds that have at least one key and overriding receptive belief. It would have to be something like my grandfather lovingly warning me as he died struggling to breathe, "never smoke." And, something in the ad was a reminder.

In other words, people can only behave or change their behavior constructively *if* their beliefs support stopping or not even starting smoking and/or vaping in the first place. The beliefs prevailing for the immature and the "I don't matter" youngsters (or even oldsters) would produce a "devil may care" attitude. Their expressed thoughts might be "oh, that won't happen to me; I'm not like those other people. I'm stronger." That type of self-expressed thought is generated by the amorally held, contrarian beliefs. One terrible outcome: The person dies a horrible death that is rooted in the belief that he or she does not matter, so what difference does being a smoker make?

Besides not mattering, what other k e y negative self-concepts d o smokers t y p i c a l l y develop based on their life experiences? I a m u n l o v a b l e , I a m a l o n e r , I h a v e t o b e p e r f e c t, I d r i v e m y s e l f r e a l h a r d, idle hands are the devil's workshop. etc. However, a single key negative, supportive of being a smoker, can be entirely unique and require core healing methodology to seek and change.

One's belief(s) always prevail, so if "good" judgment beliefs aren't hardwired in the brain, only relevant negative self concepts or beliefs will win out. If healthy beliefs are in the majority, they will shape one's judgments creating the thought that smoking or vaping isn't smart. And so, the person won't.

Once negative beliefs are hardwired, the mind must be rewired in order to operationalize good judgment. That means identifying and changing the underlying beliefs about the example of vaping/ smoking as a good idea to a set of beliefs that support the opposite. When doing that, it makes what seems to be a habit disappear. (Over the years, I have helped hundreds of smokers become nonsmokers in about two hours of work reprogramming, a sort of rewiring of their brain through the use of hypnosis to install their preferred and healthy beliefs as a supportive, empowering constellation as a non-smoker.)

Over time, a person can experience reasons why they're glad they smoke. They begin to see themselves as someone who smokes. It becomes an integral part of their persona. "I'm a smoker!"

The more reasons a person accumulates as to why they like to smoke or vape, the more "hooked" that person becomes. Those reasons as self-concepts, now a part of the brain's neural network, force the person to continue smoking/vaping — even if in a year or two they realize they made a mistake by starting. What is usually referred to as a habit is just a set of bullying, unhealthy beliefs forcing the person to continue even if now, consciously they wished they didn't.

What is true about this vaping/smoking example would be true of any "addiction," any "habit." My experience has taught me that the words "habit" and "addiction" are misused. While some substances can definitely have v e r y addictive properties, and while "positive" reinforcement can augment repeat behavior in the form of what is called "habits," the actuality is that most often it is one's negative beliefs that govern the continuance of destructive substance use and repetitive self-defeating behavior.

Learned from colleagues and by using Core Healing, the speedy, yet individualized hypnosis that I do works with most smokers, 'vapers', and tobacco chewers. (I am making this positive statement based upon the many referrals I have received.)

I estimate I have done approximately 1,000 two-hour smoking cessation sessions. Over time, the methodology has evolved based upon what doing core healing hypnosis has taught me. For example: I ask a client to do homework. "Draw a line down the middle of the page. On the left create a list of all the reasons you <u>like</u> to smoke. On the right, beside each 'like' write what you would rather do instead. Example: chew gum instead of smoking when driving. "The neighborhood centers I have dreamed about and speak about in Chapter Twelve could offer this simple approach as a community health service. It works for most. If it doesn't, then at least there's the more time consuming, investigative core healing approach that can be used.

To recap, the brain-body amorally implements one's positive *and* negative beliefs. A person's thoughts, a person's judgment concerning something like smoking/vaping is only as good as their beliefs related to it. Remember, the brain is quite simply a stimulus response mechanism actualizing beliefs that are relevant to the stimulus at hand. If I know smoking is "dumb", and, I have been convinced I am "too dumb to know better", I will smoke.

There are thousands and thousands of accumulated self-concepts and beliefs that we collect over a lifetime. Beliefs can include: self-concepts ("I am good at analyzing"); what one values (silk is the best fabric for a dressy blouse); what one has been taught and accepts as true ("an eye for an eye": I have been bullied, so now I will be the become the bully); etc. All such data is cataloged in our brains and ready to govern how we respond to any given stimulus. Thus, the more learned we are, the more actual truths accumulated, the better off we are to respond wisely, healthfully instead of just react poorly.

Stimuli that Provoke a Reaction or Response Are Received Through These Types of Bodily Receptors:

- Auditory (hearing)
- Gustatory (taste)
- Olfactory (smell)
- Visual (seeing)
- Tactile (touch)

Once a stimulus is received, it is processed at lightning speed within the individual. Responses can be of just one sort or more than one. Types of responses include: behavioral, physical, relational, spiritual and/or emotional.

Examples of unhappy types of *emotional* reactions might sound like this:

- "I'm edgy or moody."
- "I'm lonely."
- "I am anxious."
- "I am depressed."
- "I am sad."
- "I'm being obnoxious: loud and boisterous."

Alternatively, in people who are at peace with the understanding that they matter, those same stimuli can lead to a more enriched self-awareness. It can sound like this:

- "I feel so much better learning from that mistake."
- "I am happy that at least I have a friend to see me through this tough time."
- "I feel we will work things out for the better."
- "I'm glad to be able to leave that sadness behind with my desire to forgive."
- "I am feeling at peace. I don't have to shout anymore to know whether or not I am understood."

These emotions surface due to the nature of the beliefs being processed in that person's mind. *Beliefs shape how we react to everything.*

Another example, this time of a behavioral sort:
When I was young, my aunt asked, "Why do you eat so much even when you're full?" At the time it seemed like a dumb question. Had I understood then what I do now, the accurate response would be, "because that's the way we eat at home. Isn't that the way everybody eats?"

Fortunately, even though I am not trim, I am certainly fifty pounds less than I otherwise would have been. I'm blessed in that I am living a healthier and more resilient life. Finding my *truth*, my beliefs about why I was mindlessly eating so much allowed me to change my ignorant self-concepts and beliefs. Thank God my aunt asked me that question that lingered long after she said it, and eventually, I had the knowledge with which to free myself to eat more healthfully.

I want to share this knowledge with you because positive belief changes that allow for problem resolution (core healing) move you along much faster than plodding talk with self or with other analysis based upon the results of one's beliefs. The self-empowerment gained from seeking one's truths about "why" do I *actually* do what I do can be so wonderful because the results from belief truth seeking can have healthy results. That 'aha', that freeing of one's self-imposed, unwitting imprisonment due to negative self-concepts and beliefs is empowering.

Thus, the question, "how do I find out what beliefs I have accumulated that cause my being overweight?" One very important answer – hypno-analytics. Combining that with the immediate follow-up with hypnotherapy (conducted by a licensed mental health professional, not a hypnotist, per se) is the swiftest mode. Doing core healing responsibly requires much more sophisticated, comprehensive training based upon both medically and psycho-logically founded science. Working with a licensed mind-body professional who has been trained as a core healer is just plain common sense.

When the beliefs that cause the problem, in this case the problem of overeating, are identified, deleted, and replaced with better beliefs, the better beliefs will govern for a healthy approach to eating and consequent, enduring weight loss. The brain has then been "rewired."

Some clinical language to describe the process required might be:

- **S**ystematic (the hypnoanalytic discovery phase).
- **N**euro-Linguistic (with the use of language to rewire the brain)
- **R**eprogramming (the core healing phase)

Combined, they form the acronym *SNLR* which differs from NLP [neuro linguistic programing] in the sense that NLP is neither hypno-analytic nor client-centered. The NLP therapist talks with the client to determine what changes *they* think need to be made. Then do hypnotherapy. The Core Healer seeks the truth where it can be found, within the mind of the client. The truths found there provide the accurate path to healing. Therapist guesses often don't.

Raising Children for the Right Reasons

Question: Should the act of having a child be about meeting the parents' needs or about the child's needs?

In absolute terms, I doubt there is a "right" answer. *The needs and desires of both parent and baby matter.* Any reasonable conflicting interests, ideally, should be resolved *before* pregnancy.

Far too many millions, if not billions, get pregnant in a thoughtless manner. That thoughtlessness and ignorance belong to both the mother and the father. Not very often do prospective parents ask themselves any relevant or important questions regarding their readiness.

Compounding the problem — far too many lack a way to responsibly manage their sexual needs, their desire to become a parent, and access to preventing unintended, undesired pregnancy. The real crisis here is about ignorance, rape, and abuse of women's rights to prevention and therapeutic D&Cs.

Incredibly, I recently read about a country that is considering enacting a man's right to rape women. No women's and certainly no children's lives are advocated for there!

That country's world is what I refer to as the "mondo canne" or dog-eat-dog type. Love is a dead concept under those circumstances. Those men don't realize that their frightful loneliness, such as experienced by the so-called "incels" or "involuntary celibates," is because *they are so clueless as to how to be lovable.* Orgasm is their only way to assuage the anxiety their bodies experience and therefore cause even more erections. These men understand that they are in pain but not the truth of the "why" as presented here. Thus, they blame women, not their unhealthy circumstances or their negative upbringing, for their lack of understanding what it means to act like a lovable man.

People living in a country where sexual abuse is condoned, are all victims. When men such as these are raised with the self-concept of "only I matter; you women don't", they suffer too with the loss of quality, loving relationship. They are prone to indifference to the suffering they cause themselves and others. I call their approach to life empty, meaningless and pathetic pain-sharing.

Concerns that people should consider before becoming parents include:
  • Will my child survive, or even thrive, under our current circumstances?

- Am I financially secure enough to raise a child?
- Am I reasonably mentally and physically healthy enough, including not prone to depression, anxiety, raging anger, being domineering or mean, hateful and spiteful, etc., and am I obese? (Stanford University has worthwhile research on this issue of obesity. It seems it is not genetic predisposition.)
- Or, in positive terms, do I and my spouse live *loved-based, non-dogmatic beliefs*?

Literally billions of babies are born into ignorant and self-serving situations with one key maternal belief. "I fear I'll wind up all alone and not be taken care of in my senior years unless I have a child to care for me." My research with willing, female clients who were mothers showed they all had children for this reason. It is about primal, fear based survival. It can be over-ridden with wise love based survival strategies.

Another belief discovered is: "At least I'll have a child who loves me." It's the solution for the woman who sees herself as unlovable. The irony is with that belief that likely she will succeed. Her child won't love her.

Far too many children are born in thoughtless circumstances. Such rationale can be as simple as: "Having a family is what I am supposed to do. After-all, what is life without a family?" Then, there can be the desire to please one's parents so that they become grandparents. Or, it can be because they were an only child and want their child to have better circumstances by having many siblings. These unfortunate reasons for introducing children into the world perpetuate suffering for all involved. Fortunate children come into the world more altruistically, thoughtfully, preparedly.

People who believe children truly matter – not just themselves – go about having a child differently. They have a child or two. They get pregnant when they are ready to be responsible. It's not about "hovercraft parenting." It is about taking on this immense responsibility lovingly, kindly, and *with the time* to be there attentively because they are free to do so and want to do so. Such parents have the basic learnings and the financial planning to do as good a job as they can all the while living their truth: there is no such thing as a perfect parent.

People with a propensity to embrace the "I matter" self concept will more likely enact a purposeful life based on some way they've been inspired. "Good" parents, "good" clergy, "good" teachers, "good" relatives, "good" neighbors, exemplify love-based, not fear-based, beliefs and living. For more on this, please read author Sharlee Glenn's writings about her concept of ethical governance.

We Are What We Are Raised to Believe We Are

If we're raised to believe that we simply don't matter and are therefore worthless, life becomes painfully meaningless. Additionally, when raised to believe in unwholesome doctrines, some of those types of beliefs stifle or can allow snuffing out the life of another with indifference.

Many people raised in families that prescribe to a doctrine of sin and damnation end up staying with those fear-based, punishment-based, and worse yet vengeance-based beliefs but some come to "see the light." Even those that leave that belief system can still carry some beliefs in related constellations. They can suffer from embedded beliefs that have prolonged illness producing effects. And they have no knowledge of this cause and effect relationship. This book information can help free people from the unhealthy effects of such unwholesome, imprinted beliefs.

If with good fortune, you grew up in a loving family, a more wholesome, accepting culture, and were guided to believe that you mattered equally, your brain then collects supportive evidence. It then stores potential beliefs such as:

- "I'm worthy."
- "I'm intelligent."
- "I'm capable."
- "I am good enough."

If we grow up in a family that has trouble expressing love and qualifies their love and acceptance of us, we store a different set of beliefs.

"I'm worthy *if* I do all my chores correctly and never make a mistake."

"I'm intelligent *if* I get straight A's like my cousin Sandy."

"I'm capable *if* I am great at sports and get trophies and scholarship money."

That *if* is a 'killer'. It dulls the richness potential of the "you matter" in everyone.

Belief systems are learned, and yes, they do govern your behavior in an amoral fashion without any sense of right or wrong, good or bad. One's conscious judgment is governed by their beliefs. Good judgment can _only_ be implemented with the permission of supportive beliefs. If negative beliefs are governing, and you do not like their effects, they must be identified using rigorous self-analysis or better yet hypno-analytics. Then they can be found, competently deleted and replaced in order to exercise "good" judgment.

The Top 10 Love-Based Beliefs (Wellness Producing)

Throughout the history of humankind, love, being loving, and being loved are extolled, and, for so many good reasons.

There was a time when, on an elementary school field trip, the bus driver tuned into a station that played a soothing style of music. The song "Nature Boy" sung by Nat King Cole came on. I was in a relaxed state and with belief receptivity of the very young a particular message stuck. Over my lifetime, it has had a great impact on me. The words: "The greatest thing you'll ever learn is how to love and be loved in return." That lyric stuck with me. It became a learned belief that guided further learning as to how to improve my caring ability. I remember as I got older saying to myself: "I want to become the best lover I can be." With that, my definition of what it meant to be a "lover" – in the best and fullest sense of that word – became a lifelong journey.

On such a learning journey, it became clear that there are two ways to survive. One is love-based and the other hate-based. The safer way is love based. It better assures wellness in terms of our funda-mental hardwiring for survival. In part, that's why I think horri-fying art forms shouldn't be tolerated by the public. They do leave the wrong kind of blueprints, the "dangerous to self and others" type. It's not a free speech issue but one of common sense.

The way we go about surviving depends upon the beliefs of the culture in which we were raised, what was perceived, what we were taught. Such culture includes our parents primarily, their reli-gion(s), the regions, communities, schools, our country and even perceptions of our world.

Yes, we will survive one way or another. One way is in a "mondo canne" dog-eat-dog oppressive way that is the fashion throughout history in dictatorships and certain monarchies. Regrettably, it is a front and center issue in our world again today.

The other form of survival is love-based. Titans of industry, as well as monarchical dictatorships have tended to exclude this form of compassionate survival for all. Thank goodness for the study done at a company that moved financially out of the red and into the black over a period of four years. A book about it is *Everybody Matters* demonstrating the economic, lucrative power of loving respect that I call Humanomics. (Am not sure who first came up with that wonderful word.)

Surviving lovingly does not mean being naïve. We all need a host of savvy skills such as the basics of contracts, accounting, social assertiveness and even something like martial arts to survive in the real world today.

Regrettably, few if any institutions *require* we actually learn the skills of loving plus ethical but definitely survival-based living. No wonder our children of today are so scared. They are quite assuredly ill-equipped.

Top 10 Love/Competency Based Beliefs (Mental/Physical Wellness Producing)

To foster love-based living, children must be raised with several key "self" concepts:

- I matter.
- I am lovable.
- I have worth.
- I am an equal . . . no better than . . . nor less than.
- I am good enough and am able to wisely choose where I need to improve.
- I do my best.
- I am good at learning from my failures and mistakes, so I don't fear responsibility.
- I kindly care about others.
- I am capable and deserve to be heard not just seen.
- And, if one believes in God, God loves and I love, unconditionally. We share the bounty of such unifying, bliss filled Energy.

Love-based beliefs bring a wholesome sense of joy and peace.

Top 10 Hate/Fear Based Beliefs (Mental/Physical Illness Producing)

Sadly, some parents foster both mental and physical illness by exemplifying and teaching the self concepts they learned. The result is sociopathic, hate-based, mentally ill, uncaring conduct from a child as they grow up. Expressions of this include:

• I don't matter or don't matter unless I am tough, invincible, a liar, macho, and so forth.

• I am unlovable. (Over the years, having worked with about a thousand smokers, for most, if not all, this feeling of being unlovable winds up making smoking seem like a good idea. Contrary to popular notion, it is not nicotine that hooks them. Hundreds have left my office with zero withdrawal problems. The belief that nicotine is addictive is perhaps somewhat true, but more importantly it becomes just another negative belief excusing the conduct. Additionally, it creates an inner struggle when trying not to smoke. Reinforced is the identity: I am addicted. I am a smoker. And, obviously what can't addicts do? Quit easily!

• I'm not good enough. I'm inadequate, or worse, worthless.

• I'm a failure.

• I fear God. (The ancient Hebrew word for fear can be interpreted as: in awe of. Awe of God is love/wellness based. Fear of God fosters illness and hate-based vulnerability.)

• Punishment/vengeance is just and good.

• I am entitled to do whatever I please. I just have to learn the ways to get away with it.

• I am superior.

• I dominate.

• I don't care about you, just me and mine.

Hate-based, illness-based self-concepts and beliefs, which are the actual source of observed evil, bring war, death, ugliness, depression, physical illnesses, criminality, cruelty, anxiety, addictions, loveless relationships, anxiety, depression, slavery and misery often escaped by suicide, and murder. Why tolerate mental illness?

People become conflicted and exhausted when raised with a mixture of "good" and "bad." I liken it to the discomfort of sitting on a picket fence deciding between being "good" or "evil." There is no peace in that position, only profound, penetrating discomfort.

What I wish for you is what I did for myself. When I decided to "get off that fence" on the side of seeing myself as basically and fundamentally good, I became in harmony with the "good" gene that is now seen as one with which we are created. Those of you needing to do so, too, in one sense it is just that simple to accomplish. Again, remember, it is about direction not perfection. Improving is the direction.

Now, getting on the side of the fence where we all actually belong was like going through a gateway. It allowed that "good" gene to be in the "on" position [read later about Epigenetics, a new field of study, in Chapter Twelve]. That means that the ability to begin a heightened sense of lovability is supported genetically. It became not just my gateway to the goodness type living but also to the ability to experience Heaven on Earth. That's not because I was perfect — anyone who knows me knows I am not — but because I was free to lovingly do my best as a humane being, and that matters. (The word "humane" is meant to communicate the exercise of our human wellness-based qualities. For example, during the dark days of the Coronavirus pandemic, we have witnessed the *humaneness* of the multitudes and diversity of our "everyday heroes." It was not just thrilling to have the opportunity to watch TV night after night with these types of news reports but to witness the creativity, the bravery and the generosity of spirit of the varied, ever-so-creative, marvelous acts of kindness.)

And the reward? It is the holy, humbling communion with the reality of God. I assure you we are not alone. We just need to raise our children to be lovingly available to actualize their goodness, their mattering, their lovability, and then that comforting reality becomes faithfully available.

❄

Please never forget. Parenting must be considered a privilege. Our government could offer incentives supportive of healthier parenting. Incentavization could be implemented legally (with great forethought and carefully designed parameters) as reward for those who have demonstrated an equality, kindness, responsibility orientation in their everyday conduct.

One idea: enact four different types of marriage licenses.

1. A three year marriage license that lapses. It may be renewed.
2. A family marriage license that gives government benefits such as tax reductions to:
   those married for three years, no DUIs, no domestic violence reports, a minimum of one year's worth of savings, no surrogate, hand-off parenting such as nannies for a child's first 5 years of life (except after the fact as in the death of a parent, and as an example, a grandparent helps out), and both parents demonstrate they are typically, physically and psychologically fit to parent. (Physical handicaps are not a problem so long as safety of child care can be demonstrated.)
3. A marriage license after the lapsed one with no fitness requirements but no tax or other government benefits for the couple or for any children they may have.
4. A senior citizen marriage license with government benefits for those 68 and older.

3

"I'm Fine" - Really?

THE FIVE W's come from the basic questions a journalist asks when interviewing someone for an article. They are: who, what, where, when and why. If you can answer these five questions about any event, anything you are trying to learn about, you will have the guts of the story.

In my core healing work, the most critical of the five is the last of them, the word "why". It requires the mightiness of truth seeking. And regardless of whether we like seeing clichés in writing, the often-used Biblical concept "seek the truth, it sets you free" is definitely the right approach from a core healing perspective.

If we seek to understand *why* we do something, we have to get to the core beliefs causing our actions. We must drill down using hypno-analytics to arrive at the real "why." Rarely does your conscious mind know the truth, let alone the whole truth.

Obviously, and for example, we don't have language in utero or even when we reach one to two years of age. However, an infant can initially feel agitated or calm, wanted or unwanted. Depending on what is being sensed, a fetus will feel calm, in tranquil amniotic fluid and with stress-free hormone transmission. That infant's experience, the feeling of safety and especially sense of being loved, fosters the gurgling little newborn. The feeling of *You Matter* can originate there as a self-concept and flourish if nourished accordingly.

If the child was born with the immediate sense of being unsafe, unwanted, or not cared about, there is an anxiety imprint because the fundamentals of survival are threatened. So, whether we feel welcomed or not — meaning we matter or not — proves a significant factor in self-care and our caring about others. Thus, as one's belief system evolves from felt senses into representational words, a person will be guided along one of four paths:

- I matter equally.
- I don't matter *unless*, or, *only if* I ____ (fill in the blank: a prominent one for many being "have children").
- I don't matter at all.
- Only I matter.

Approximately eighty percent of the answers to your "why" questions emerge from the descriptive language of your felt senses about who you are and how you perceive yourself regarded over the course of your first six years of life. For example, here was one of mine: "Well, I guess I just don't matter." For me, this conclusion was arrived at because my birth parents didn't want me. I was adopted. With immature logic, the resulting self-concepts and beliefs became: "I must not be lovable. . . . I must not be good enough. . . . I must be ugly."

Now, not all adoptees arrive at exactly the same conclusions about self. Those were mine. As an aside, you can imagine how those beliefs made me a handful for my adoptive parents.

Thus, it is correct to say, a high percentage of your self-concepts and beliefs, such as those of mine, were derived so young , and, in the language of the child self, they were *not* consciously remembered but quite troublesomely enacted.

That is true for us all. Most beliefs generating our problems —
and also those supportive of our strengths — are unknown
to one's own conscious awareness. They are simply enacted
seemingly out of nowhere and at times mistakenly attributed
to: "It's in my genes."

Additional self-concepts and beliefs accumulate throughout one's
lifetime. Those self-concepts and beliefs are more in the language
of an adult. One devastating one is: "I have to be perfect." Most of
us, as adults, rationalize that of course as humans we know perfection is not always possible. However, the amoral mind implements
your definition of perfection *and* its relative urgency to you. A
manic episode is a perfectionism attempt on steroids — regrettably
because whatever that person does is judged by the self as "not
good enough." The depression that follows is often the "escape
hatch." Lying in bed is a release from the exhaustion of the effort
and allows for escape and recovery. A psychotic episode is another
form of escape from an intense fear of failure.

Thus, our amoral minds implement the beliefs of the individual for
better or for worse, in sickness and in health. That is why we do
things that can be wise or can instead be harmful to our bodies,
our minds, and our spirits. Let's consider an example.

Question: "Why do I eat so much unhealthy fast food?"

Here are conscious responses followed by subconsciously derived
truth:

• *Because I don't have time to eat otherwise.*

Actual reason: I don't matter enough to take the time to find and
learn to enjoy eating at a restaurant that serves healthier food.

• *It's easy and tastes so good.*

Actual reason: Dad didn't like mom's cooking. So, more often than
not we ate takeout that Dad picked up on the way home from
work. Dad often got my favorite of some kind of piled-high

burgers like a bacon burger. I felt special and loved when eating such food.

• *Because it's cheap and all I can afford since cigarettes keep getting more expensive.*

Actual reason: I'm not worth it. I don't matter.

Fortunately, the true answers to the issues we humans have can be discovered and resolved with core healing. And even though such hazardous identities as exemplified above can prevail, better ones can replace them and become actualized. Better yet, we can learn how to raise our children more wisely, seeing the consequences of our potentially harmful, unwittingly imprinted beliefs that can govern each child as an adult for the worse.

Thus, the answers to a question such as "Why do I eat so much (unhealthy) fast food," are beliefs that can have terrible consequences. Not only don't we take better care of ourselves but, by extension, our planet doesn't matter enough either. So much of our world's tragedies go back to the key and damagingly consequential belief held by far too many of us at core, which sadly is: "I don't matter" or "I don't matter enough to bother."

Seek the Truth – It Will Set You Free

People are amazed, they are blown away, when in a state of heightened awareness, they hear themselves speak their *actual* truth in answer to their own "why" questions. Through such a state of awareness, whether brought about through the preferred use of a professional using hypnosis or a guided meditative means, people can discover a great deal about themselves. For example, they can find out that they feel like a much bigger failure than they realized. Importantly, they can learn the true "why" behind their beliefs. Amazement grows still further when they rid themselves of the identities that historically led them to a sense of being a failure and related feelings of weakness, unhappiness, and anxiety.

The core healing process allows a person to be free to actualize the empowerment that comes by *learning* from one's derived errors in judgment. It's like a weight is lifted off their shoulders. Moreover, realizing that a former self-concept such as "I am just plain stupid" is being replaced by "now I am free to love learning" is life changing. The consequence of acting stupidly by being ignorant, when replaced with loving learning, opens opportunities to utilize new knowledge and gain the joy of succeeding in ways that had earlier escaped them. That is the shift that is so desperately needed by so many. When liberated in this way, they can now be informed in ways that allow for greater success rather than more failure.

How Do We Get Where We'd Rather Be

As indicated above, truth-seeking is greatly facilitated through the use of hypnosis. Some people use meditation. Typically, however, these approaches to a heightened awareness state are used for different purposes. When one wants to empty their mind by just focusing on their breathing, for example, that is referred to as meditation. When one wants to actively seek their truth in a heightened awareness and recollective state, hypno-analytics is the mode of choice.

Do read more about Meditation in Chapter Twelve. Shared there is one man's journey of learning and using it. That story is shared because meditation is being shown to have a marvelously wonderful, major capacity for healing. Neighborhood wellness centers need to offer both core healing and meditation but additionally other supportive healing forms such as medical, nutritional, and educational. Again, that all is addressed in Chapter Twelve.

From a core healing standpoint, when one wants to change in order to behave in healthy, uplifting ways *and* feel calm, happy and at peace sooner than later, that is when the heightened awareness state called for is hypnosis. In addition, what is recognized with this approach is that *the truth* required to resolve a person's problems *lies within* the *individual being treated.* It is not within the therapist. In professional terms it is called "client-centered therapy."

For most, but not all clients, such a truth-seeking journey into self is transformational. That is why this client-centered approach is preferred. *However,* people severely and frequently traumatized in their childhood are *not* candidates for this style of healing. Neuro-feedback or other medically oriented methodologies could be more appropriate in terms of "rewiring" the brain.

Lastly, please see core healing not just as the type of client-centered approach that can wither issues and blossom alternatives but also view it as a key to address the whole range of human problems. Those are: emotional, behavioral, physical, relational and / or spiritual challenges.

Bringing Your Truth to the Surface

Once you have embraced the act of bringing your truths to the surface and into your conscious awareness, you can begin to find harmony with the universe. Your negative memories, many as traumatized past experiences, dim when hypno-therapeutically healed using a host of psychotherapies developed since Sigmund Freud's research. When brought to the surface, pain imprints, referred to as "sore spots" can be dissolved by virtue of the core healing process. The body unburdened heals. Behaviors change. Better emotions are felt. These "sore spots" conveyed negative outcomes for the individual through historical negative beliefs. When transformed, when healed, people experience the birth of new, wholesome self-concept beliefs and related constellations' development. That new array of beliefs plus their growing, supportive constellations dictate how you behave and how you then react in any relevant situation.

As the reader, you have seen and will see further examples of how distinct negative — and positive — concepts happen. Because this book is oriented to illness prevention, you will see more examples of negative self-concept and belief development within these pages. Let me elaborate on my personal example.

My aunt, asking me why I continued to eat when I was surely full, created a start for a positive constellation of eating style beliefs. It posed a "why" that stuck with me. It informed, it imprinted in my brain that I didn't need to eat the way the rest of my family did kind of like depression era style. It helped me to eventually become aware of enough negative self-concepts and beliefs so as to more consistently curb my eating. Thus, it was a good belief and one that I was eventually free to enact. In this case the outcome eventually was positive. It could have gone very differently, if my assortment of belief constellations dismissed my aunt's input entirely.

It is also important to note at this juncture that adults are human, meaning the obvious. They make mistakes. They themselves are victims of their negative self-concept and belief imprints. So, they can perpetuate unwitting harm to children and embed in young minds their own belief systems that demonstrate the "how" of feeling depressed and anxious as well as the mis-truths, half-truths, and misconceptions that cause illness in its various forms.

A father who yells at a child, "Stop eating so much. Look how fat you're getting," could cause that child to form the deep-seated belief that they are and always will be, fat. The child may "push those words down" the way they come to push food down, and not look at that "false truth." The real truth that needs to be brought to the surface is how damaging those words were and how much they affected that child's body. *That system of beliefs actualizes their behavior to do whatever necessary for them to be fat, whether consciously they liked being fat or not.* The father's shouted words imprinted. The child who was subjected to that message needs rewiring.

Once we know how to fully "see" the entire range of aspects that come together to identify us as "fat," and surface those forces, then we can begin to dismantle the savagery of that identity. Otherwise, those issues are never resolved. They not only remain within a person throughout their entire lifetime but they govern people's health. Eventually, high blood pressure, heart disease, cancer, or viruses cause them to die as a "fat" person. That person will implement his/her definition of what their mind understood the father meant by the word "fat." That youngster will become that definition and any other beliefs that cancerously grew from it.

- "I'm stupid and worthless."
- "I can never lose weight."
- "I am unlovable."
- "I'm too ugly to have/enjoy sex."
- "I'm not worthy of a loving partner, happy healthy children, good friends."
- "I can never experience good physical health. I will ALWAYS be sickly from being so overweight."

Over time, such seemingly true beliefs accumulate. They pile on the weight beyond the misguided father's meaning. They come to appear true because they are implemented faithfully by the amoral mind. It is not habit but repeated implementation of the belief.

Their experience begins to support these beliefs, which soon take over on a conscious level. The experience of the individual is repetitive and self-evident. But such belief constellations can be found, exposed, and resolved according to each individual's constellation.

The key is to reconnect with your *whole* truth, while in a heightened state of awareness and seeing where those beliefs were created. Your brain, so to speak, can be rewired with a new set of beliefs that will automatically shift your behavior in such a way that your physical being trims down and your emotional feelings improve. Your mind will implement the new identity's parameters because the old ones have been deleted.

Now . . .

- "I'm smart and capable of eating healthfully."
- "I don't need these extra pounds. They are no longer serving me, it's good to feel free to lose them."
- "My life matters, my health matters, because I matter."
- "I love myself now, the way I have loved my children."
- "My health will now improve."

When you get in touch with *your truth*, not your spouse's, not your therapist's, you can start to resolve these issues. You can change the trajectory of your future. By seeking the knowledge of your unhealthy beliefs about self as well as others, you start to release the limitations of the false beliefs and the pain they've caused you. With the right kind of help, with these understandings about how the amoral mind works, you set the stage for and enact a better lifestyle. This kind of inside out change is *visibly* transformational.

Core Healing hypnosis facilitates the release of the limiting belief imprints that have negatively dictated the unhealthy, unkind aspects of your behavior. And, not only can you release your own suffering this way, but the suffering of those who love you and who witness your self-destructive behaviors.

Surfacing and facing the answers to your "why" questions such as: "Why *won't* I lose weight?" allows for the real possibility of eliminating such a problem. Self-sabotaging ideas created in childhood — or anywhere in your past — can be found. The attachments to such constellations of negative self-concepts and beliefs can be severed, can be deleted and replaced with far better beliefs so that the pain, confusion, anxiety, physical illness, and depression can dissipate to the point of extinction. It sounds miraculous. It can be. Also, let's imagine this kind of help.

Replacing inflammatory and immune-suppressing beliefs with enhancing ones can definitely allow for a return to, if not robust health, certainly much improved well-being. There is hope. And know that you are by no means alone in such a challenge. Based on more than thirty-five years of experience, I would venture to say that all of us suffer more or less in the ways described here. The good news: It does not have to be that way anymore. Just follow such a path to your truths. Surfacing them empowers you .

The truth leads to reformation, to beauty creation. Suddenly, things become possible, things you never considered that could be true for you do become true. See who you really are — a person who matters equally. You are nice-looking "enough." But more importantly, you are at last more than just "enough" healthy.

Remember this blessing you deserve to experience. When you begin to discover your relevant past, and start to find your truth, you can begin to change your future for the better. That's "mattering." That's becoming wholesomely influential. That is joy-filled living. Then you are fine. Really!   You'll know it.

4

Nothing Will Ever Change: Right?

WHEN WE CHAMPION WITH ONE VOICE, "ALL OUR CHILDREN MATTER EQUALLY": THERE IS HOPE

FIRST, we must ask ourselves the following "whys":

- If I am richer than you, *why* shouldn't my children have more educational advantages than yours?
- Since I am white, *why* shouldn't my children be treated as superior to yours who are not white?
- Since my religion is the right one and yours is not the best one, *why* shouldn't my children be allowed to "reign"?
- Since I was born to be physically stronger than you, *why* am I not therefore better equipped to be deemed superior by virtue of brute force?

Why have these and similar assumptions repeated throughout human history and managed to dictate the behavior of humanity?

An answer could be that we emulate and mimic the animal world. We assume since we too are animals, we live by the same code — survival of the fittest. Therefore, someone who is a colonialist, an imperialist, simply needs to find some cronies who gather together to decide who are the fittest — starting with themselves, of course. Their belief is: "only I matter". Consequently, only my faith matters, only my Book matters, only my god matters, only my country matters, etc. These subterfuges are about money and power. There is no altruism, no God, only "I matter", only I am your leader/god, only I am the one to tell you what you can or cannot do. You are the servant of my almighty, moneyed "I".

Expanding on the theme of imperialism, throughout the centuries of human history, survival of the fittest became about:

- Tamping down a man's actual fears about self-adequacy in order to survive and not simply provide for one's family.
- Power and the money necessary to be Number One, the "fittest."
- The hiring of legions: the survival-dependent soldiers, the paid enforcers under the command of the self-serving "Number One."
- One's skin color and/or religious beliefs as a mesmerizing power-broker.
- Belonging among the elite (depending upon easily identifiable indicators of assumed superiority as defined by each one's culture).

The sense of superiority gleaned from these status conveying situations calms the anxiety regarding the fear of being alone and quite particularly of not surviving.

A man may ask himself:

Am I up to the challenge of being man enough?

Am I physically equipped enough?

Am I among the strongest, smartest, richest and most clever?

The second and third statements define the first. These are the current key measures of what it means to be "man enough."

The sad shame of emulating a wolf-like model is that it fosters huge amounts of cruelty and suffering. Such model for survival of the fittest for all these thousands of years does not allow for incorporating and utilizing the ways we are, or can be, inherently superior to the animal kingdom. I call it the humane evolution revolution.

We have a far superior mode of communication with each other. We have a sophisticated ability with language that affords the potential exercise of wisdom that can reduce suffering hugely. So, this book in a sense asks: Why do we continue to live like wolves? Why live a model of survival that thrives on beliefs that foster illness? Based upon scientific research, we could *evolve* ourselves to be humanely based, by exercising wellness affording beliefs instead.

We could pursue survival in a whole new and far easier, more joy-filled way by *being humanely superior to how we may have behaved in the past.* We can learn the ways of raising ourselves and our children with the wellness beliefs provided here.

Evolve? As being suggested here? Humanely? Really? Is it doable?

Yes, it seems so. Our DNA does in fact change based upon our beliefs.(See Stanford University study regarding weight loss and whether being overweight is perceived as genetic or not.)

What that means is that collectively we are able to bring about the demise of illness/hate-based w o l f - l i k e self-concepts and beliefs, which foster fear-based living. The discomfort that creates fear and chaos is usually mismanaged and significantly contributes to despair and early death.

Innately, we yearn for a healthful, more secure, and quite confident mode of living in order to survive. A major block to this kind of living is the belief, "I don't matter" only 'he' does, like one's father.

If, on the other hand, we grow up believing "I matter equally," our innate demands can lead to living more healthfully and with joy in the manner that love can foster. Now that we know what interferes with that normalcy, we are able to "write" love-based living into our genetic code over time. That's why I am so excited about what I have learned from collecting hypno-analytic data during all of these decades. This knowledge championed in the unification of our wellness-oriented voice, can lead to creating a world that is worth being born into. With one voice, supporting the raising of our children with a sense of equality, with one voice that says each of us matters, we can lay the foundation for powerful, wholesome, evolutionary forces to come into play.

In that truth there is hope.

And so, I ask:

Do you want to reflect on these ideas? Are you free to imagine the difference that mattering equally could make if historical fears and the enslaving, wolf-like worldview were replaced and negative, illness-producing beliefs were buried?

Because if you are free enough, you'll know that overall wellness in a nurturing world is doable when a heartfelt and wise commitment to equality prevails. And, it is just plain smart to make life neighborly. We are witnessing right at this very moment in time the gloriousness of millions of "Mr. Rogers" figures, both male and female, in our neighborhoods.

Hope and healing benefits will blossom in those hearts, the hearts of the "good," the "love-based" folks. The more people who begin to see and to live these benefits, the healthier our people and our planet will become.

When the prevailing voice in your belief system is a loving voice, wisdom's voice, freedom's voice saying *You Matter*, then promoting equality can become a way of life. It provides for the survival of the fittest in an entire new way. Wellness, happiness, loving kindness — these make survival much easier, joyful, and relatively anxiety free. Imagine the difference such an idea could make. Take the time to evaluate during the coming days and weeks, as different events occur and different contexts arise in which to reflect on these ideas about mattering kindly.

On May 8, 2020 you may have been fortunate to tune into a twenty-four hour long 'streamathon' on TV titled: "The Call to

Unite." It was the brainchild of Tim Shriver, another everyday hero reaching out encouraging "hugs"(even if for now just elbow ones. During the show, people like GW Bush , Oprah, and YoYo Ma appeared. Just think about it, that array of guests in and of themselves speak volumes for Equality with a capital E. (As I may have mentioned, my definition for God is an unconditionally loving Energy. So, that is why the capital E for equality. It is the sharing of God Energy. For more information, the website is: Unite.us)

In the last analysis, the question becomes: How do you want to live? Love-based or hate-based? Without prejudice or with prejudice? There's no sitting on the fence. Do you want to be among the brute force, chaos, and fear-engendering, climate change denying, self-serving imperialists of today's world?

Or would you prefer to live what I call mental health's prescriptive prophecy of being "among the meek," meaning: among the gentle, the kind, the nonviolent? Being among the meek is wisdom's way, the humane evolution's way.

The Decision to Change

All change starts with the decision to change. Many might fear making such an awesome decision as called for here. Making a responsible decision risks being at fault. Being at fault for those fearing fault has meant that punishment awaits. With the threat of punishment comes the desire to escape the pain. Hence, change can lead to a fear of being responsible.

But what if, with this very important prospect of the major wellness benefits realized when all matter equally, we let down our guard on those fears? Yes, during a period of transition some negatives, even dangerous ones can occur. But, with steadfastness, we work through those transitional times. Wanting our children to reap the benefits of comfortability with the notion of equality, eventually in chorus, they will be free to say to each other: *YouMatter.*

The fact is, acting superior to one another does not make the world a safer place. Just the opposite.

Alternatively, what if you believe nothing can ever change? That means your belief hasn't allowed you to register what has changed for the better in our world, such as improving the quality of life for many by making sure people don't starve during this pandemic. That means a person gets to live longer and healthier. Allow yourself to hear that truth. Allow yourself to say it out loud, yes that is true, life has been extended for the better for many because everyday heroes are implicitly saying a n d e n a c t i n g everybody matters.

Now, make this commitment. Write it down. Post it where you can see it.

1. Everyone matters equally and importantly including myself.
2. I will find my way to help make humane mattering happen.
3. United, we can do this.
4. Past negative history will not define who I choose to be now.

Your choice otherwise is to do what I call "living in vinegar." It's the life of a cynic. Cynics l e a r n t o become bitter when they haven't achieved their goals. And, based on world history, the goal I am suggesting might seem impossible. But it no longer remains impossible. So drop the pessimistic lens through which you may have been looking. That lens distorts your vision. You can't change for the better until you commit yourself to be better as a hope oriented being. (Depression lessens as a result.)

By living the core wellness beliefs found in the Glossary and else-where in this book, you can make evolutionary history for the better and your own life sweeter in the process. That may sound pretty wild, but I invite you to keep your mind open to what you are learning here. I have witnessed such transformation often.

Here is an example of such transformation from among those we are accustomed to thinking of as "they have it all." That growing group of terribly troubled young people are described as well-to-do, white, generally wealthy college students, primarily male. Depression, anxiety, plus drug and alcohol dependencies, are so out of hand in this group that their lives are 'on the line.'

The very caring, well to do parents of such a student asked me if I'd work with their daughter. They were scared for her life. She fit the category of this group based upon her presenting problems but with the obvious exception of course being she was not a he. Similarly, however, she felt terribly lost under the pressures to cope with the overwhelming degree of fundamental primal issues in today's seemingly apocalyptic world. Racing thoughts, dread and despair were her norm too.

 Like the others, this young woman saw herself so burdened with unrealistic expectations that all she could foresee was failure. Feelings of not being smart enough to pass the course work, get a stable, well-paying job, have a place to live she could afford on her own upon graduation, inadequacy as marriage material, weakness, perfectionism, even bad and deserving of punishment, etc., contributed to her tailspin of being anxiety-ridden and out of control.

For such young people today, succeeding in the free-for-all of so many challenging circumstances, survival in today's academic, technological, social and business world has been overwhelming with huge pressures they are ill-equipped by nature to manage. Nature has been put out of balance by a host of circumstances happening all at the same time.

First of all, there is the majorly miscalculated consequence of the 'bottom line' devotion. Work is the master, people the slave to it.

For many, the richer you are, the more of a success, the greater your power, the higher the respect due you. And all if you just want it badly enough, if you are willing to work hard enough and long enough. No wonder this young lady and thousands of others struggling with academic and life's anticipated pressures find themselves in the anxiety/depressive drug dependent mess she found herself in. Who wouldn't want to escape a life that seems so overwhelming?

The positive aspects of this young woman's parenting majorly helped to empower her core healing journey to wellness. She now sees herself as strong of inner character, responsible, and compassionate. She is no longer using psychotropic medications. (She was "titrated properly," which is extremely important.) With her life, she wants to teach by example this message: "no matter how tough the problem, you are bigger than your problems." Then she goes on to say: "being growth-oriented succeeds ultimately."

That's this woman's wise decision. Where change is needed she will be tenacious in dealing with it. The framing of her decision to change is a decision to ongoing growth. That too was very wise of her. She will find trying times ahead. It goes with the territory of life. But her commitment to growth will continue regardless of what future struggles occur. She will transcend with such tenacity.

Now regarding the decision for change broadening its scope from the individual to the universal survival issues at hand. In a world that commits itself to everybody matters equally, once that commitment is made country by country, we vote to make sure we are prepared to prevent or minimize disasters to the extent possible. Our Earth is it. Mars is not home. Colonists who might settle there will take undermining beliefs with them that will ultimately make it uninhabitable. There's no running away. There's no hiding. You can't start anew with 'old' you. "Heal ourselves. Heal our children. Together, we will be equipped to heal the world".

United, we need not allow civilization to become mere dust on a dead planet. That is what the paralyzing, self-serving inaction that is associated with not mattering does for life and legacy. *It doesn't have to be that way.* We can make those four core commitments. (p53)

Those four commitments to wholesome mattering do not require you to become King Kong thumping your chest in order to matter and to ward off danger. It is up to us to actively grow a united, humane bond for kindness with self and others in a world that outlaws the fear and chaos vendors. They are the ones we see and hear in tabloid "news'" outlets. They are maggots that make a fortune feeding off of us.

Know your enemy. They are the self-serving, tell-any-lie-you-want disruptors, the perpetrators of mondo canne. Their message is akin to one yelling: "Fire, fire, run" in a crowded theater where there is no fire. They're just having fun "exercising their First Amendment Rights." Really? That's only in the mondo canne worldview. That is not free speech. It is cruel, inhumane speech. It's "killer speech."

Now, let us remember instead the heart-warming stories that we see often at the end of a nightly news broadcast. If there are enough of us living love-based versus fear-based lives, supporting humane living and eventual humane evolution, we will have the bonus of more than planet salvation we will have heaven on Earth.

"Love thy neighbor as thyself." *You Matter.* They matter equally as do you. With that in mind, unite to live the four commitments. That will make change easier because you know where you are headed to make this vastly important difference. For a marvelous example of Earth-loving salvation, I would recommend the website www.worldwarzero.com.

Twenty-First Century Survival Blueprint: Becoming a Change Agent
The principles you are being guided toward living stand in accord with the following wellness blueprint. What follows is not just

another list of beliefs but a list to be welcomed according to the parenthetical guidelines. The more of us who make the decision to be love-based versus fear-based, the more and more of us who will enjoy wellness living. And, educated thusly, there will be more of us who will be able to reduce suffering not just for ourselves but for others whose lives surround ours.

Mentioned earlier, an additional major bonus in such a shift is the very salvation of our Mother Earth. It will thrive with love and care. Otherwise, we have a planet of the scared, survival threatened rapists versus the Evolved. The Evolved are not just the very humane and cuddly ones *but also the ones who will be exceptional when utilizing defensive and clever tactical measures for any types of existential attack.*

A CHANGE AGENT'S BLUEPRINT:

Decision 1: Mattering (healthfully mattering to yourself and mattering to others)

Decision 2: Loving kindness (the "good self" prevailing)

Decision 3: Equality (embraced / unreservedly)

Decision 4: Non-violent (punishing banned; humane correction embraced). Learn skilled self defense. Girls too!

Decision 5: Actualizing / developing your inherent strengths for the common good as well as for self-defense.

Decision 6: Wellness / resilience / celebratory / youthful type living.

Decision 7: Honesty.

Decision 8: Embracing responsibility.

Decision 9: Pacing to allow for the exercise of one's personal best as good enough.

Decision 10: Lover of learning.

As one voice, we can unite decisively for such skill development and exemplification, in our homes, our schools, our communities, our houses of worship. All are logical places to hone the supportive skills needed to enact Decisions 1 through 10 *from the "get-go" of existence.* Often, you'll hear me say: "It's absolutely not about perfection but quality of direction."

This blueprint for the most critical values to live, breathe, exemplify to "walk the walk," and live with peace within — as actualizing and wholesome change agents — becomes quite doable. By the way, did you notice the overlap of blueprint values as agents for change dovetailing with those of love-based versus hate-based self-concepts and beliefs? They are a matter of mattering, *of life and death.*

Change Is Easier: When You Let Go of Fear-based Living

What is so bad about fear? Don't we want our children to be afraid of us so they'll do what we tell them if for no other reason than to keep them safe? That answer can be seen as one of those yes and no situations. Perhaps yes until such time as they get 'it' meaning actualizing safety imprints. In other words, perhaps yes, until such time as they have learned how to keep themselves safe and out of trouble and make friends. Perhaps yes, until they are old enough to know they can trust us.

The no part of the answer of using fear based, screaming based, corporal punishment methods to keep a little child safe has to do the danger of instilling fear for purposes of obeying. While fear instilling can lead to obeying you, fear also leads to anger, potential rebellion and, at its worst abdication of authority for self. Thus, is there a better way?

The issue then becomes one of: *what's the better way?* How should this kind of immediacy of response, for safety reasons, be generated until such time as the child can be increasingly safe based upon developing the skills necessary for managing a host of threats to safety and well being?

There are two basic ways. Sternness of tone and bearing plus preparation by taking the time to train a child to have *no* mean <u>*no*</u>. This path is endorsed for mental and physical wellness development.

Keeping a child 'in line' has a tone of negativity. So, to be clear, the unhealthy ways h a v e t o d o w i t h parents acting inconsistent and pain-inflicting (meaning some degree of violence, such as "smacking"). This parental style perpetuates violence to self, one's future children, and to the 'other'.

Using these negative modes of parenting during a child's life imprints in the child's brain the development of unhealthy self-concepts and beliefs such as:

Oh, my parents don't really care if I get hurt (wishy-washy).

I can get away with risky behavior when Dad (or Mom) has had a bad day at work (inconsistent).

I'm only safe if I have someone there to smack me when I'm tempted to act in risky ways (fear yet embrace of authoritarianism's pain).

Often — as wild as this may sound, unless of course you are someone who does this to yourself — people will smack them-selves when no one is around to do it for them.

In order to get rid of fear-based living, it's important to understand that fear-based beliefs are developed by example, t h r o u g h traumatizing experiences, imitation, humiliation and name-calling.

They include:

- Calling a child "shy," a large factor leading to addictions.

- Misusing food as comfort and going to the fridge as distraction from discomforting feelings.
- Vengeance as pain management. It's the discharge of pain. It is also what I call pain sharing as pain relieving.
- Escaping self-responsibility (the fear of the consequences for being at fault).
- Being a couch potato to escape life while watching television, or a smoker to force the self to take a break (I won't be lovable or acceptable unless I am perfect). Over
- or under exercising to escape or escalate fears. Learning to
- "depress"*** (e.g., staying in bed and using sleep as escape).

[***Dr. William Glasser introduced the idea that the nouns "depression" and "anxiety," when enacted, could be a decision to depress or to anxiety. Depressing can, for example, be used as some type of "secondary gain," like the escape from perfectionism's behavioral exhaustion. It was Dr. Glasser (no relation of mine) who introduced the notion that those nouns become verbs when he described "Choice Theory" in the 1970s. Some aspects of his theory we now know to be erro-neous but other aspects have proven correct.]

These learned fear/anxiety management and self-concept modes lead to diseases such as: high blood pressure, stroke, chronic obstructive pulmonary disease (COPD), cirrhosis of the liver, drug addiction, cancer, suicide, and early death by the ensuing consequences of such a lifestyle.

By the way, instead of ever calling children "shy," tell them they are wisely cautious around strangers. Why? A major reason is that "shy" people turn to the dis-inhibiting effect of cannabis, alcohol, and drugs to allow themselves to socialize rather than experience the pain of loneliness. Shy, as a belief about self, means not trusting and being scared of others. Those beliefs lead to self-isolation. Then too, shy smokers often use cigarettes as "safe" companions to calm the painful feelings of being alone. The irony is being alone without caring companionship is counter to the optimal opportunity for surviving. The fear of being alone is "numero uno" on the fear chart of innate beliefs. All humans, unless trained for the ability to embrace and manage solitude, fear being alone. Survival is threatened in that State. So it becomes logical that survival is augmented and fear subsides with significant others, supportive units, groups, and families. We crave the well being, the sense of safety of being truly loved . What I call the 'I am loved' hormone, provides a marvelous natural 'high'.

Compassion, Forgiveness and Self-Awareness Lead the Way for Change

COMPASSION

I am awed. Stanford University has a whole department teaching and conducting research in regard to the employment of caring and compassion. [http://ccare.stanford.edu]

The importance of caring, without which there can be no compassion, is the difference between someone with an antisocial personality disorder, meaning one who is harmful to the welfare of others, and one who likely is not.

Compassion fosters empathy. Compassion is the skilled application of walking in another person's shoes. It allows one the wise exercise of being "among the meek," the gentle and the kind. The importance of compassion is huge for fostering peace on Earth.

Compassion is essential in the fostering of wellness both mentally and physically. The exercise of empathy/compassion can rapidly reduce anger and consequently fear. Inherently, that allows for enhancing loving relationships. People feel safer in an anger-free environment. Anger reduction has another benefit. It is an internal anti-inflammatory which physically makes one healthier. Also, when people exhibit less anger, fear-based reactions are reduced. Reducing fear minimizes the challenge to the immune system. These two key systems account for your physical wellness in major ways.

Cancer is inflammatory related. High blood pressure can also be fostered with anger. Heart attacks caused by smoking to suppress anger is a significant source of death. Bottom line: The ability to exercise caring, empathy, and compas-sion fosters love, which fosters survival in a way that makes being alive a joy.

FORGIVENESS

Forgiveness means "letting go of pain and anger." When I read that definition in the dictionary, I decided I wanted to be the fastest forgiver in town. Be assured, that does not mean I want to continue to hang out with a nasty, vengeful, irresponsible person when I forgive them. It just means I won't dwell; I refuse to dwell in the pain and the anger with their betrayal.

I like feeling well. I don't like living in the churn of "dis-ease" meaning not being or feeling at ease.

SELF-AWARENESS

Once you experience the freedom and the serenity that your self-awareness of your truths bring, and once you experience that whatever bad-outcome mistakes you make *are not your fault*, then you are free to exercise what *is* your responsibility. Your responsi-bility is not fearing those mistakes. Your responsibility is fixing them. Your responsibility is getting over being mad at the person who caused you the grief of the beliefs they engendered within you and the awful consequences to you all those years ago.

There is no Pandora's jar for us to quiver about. It does not exist within. We do not need to fear our unknowns. They are not our fault. They are knowable. And, using guided hypno-analytics we can know what needs knowing, be freed to wholesomely change and make peace with that which needs forgiving.

Always remember, you were born purely good. "Bad" people are raised that way — badly. Use this book for re-raising yourself in better ways, the ways that you need. Use this book to raise your children, our villages' children, with a heightened awareness and integration of the wellness self-concepts and beliefs.

Raise yourself up, and raise your children to readily exercise compassion with self and others, with forgiveness for self and others, and with increasing self-awareness over the years of your life.

Again, it's about wellness direction not perfection. *You Matter.*

❄

5

Actualizing Hope: Begin Here
THE INDICATORS OF MATTERING

HERE ARE twelve key indicators that tell us whether you believe subconsciously that you are worthy of life, that you indeed matter even to a reasonable degree. Generally, the imprints that determine whether you matter are made on your brain early in life and into your teens. Your actions verify, or do not verify, mattering.

1. You are alive. (Assuming at birth you are not genetically predisposed to early death or later environmentally sickened.)

2. Generally speaking, you are healthy.

3. You do not engage in risky activity.

4. You live a purposeful life with some degree of joy and passion.

5. Your style is youthful.

6. There are people in your life to whom you sincerely matter.

7. You are able to admire your own self-improvement efforts. (It's not about being egotistical but rather appreciative of the growth in your accomplishments. It's about feeling good enough because you are improving in ways you deem important).

8.   Being competitive and winning seem less and less important as you age. Existence isn't about living life as a contest but simply mattering to self and others lovingly.

9.   Primarily, your life is not about the exercise of power over others, which is all too often at their expense. Rather, you readily accept responsibility with ease and with decency.

10.   You earn, save and contribute to common community causes.

11.   You find learning and sharing fun.

12.   Regardless of the religion in which you were raised, or in which your family is affiliated, you are free to entertain the idea and joy of participating in the sharing of the awesomeness of God's Loving Energy.

In my own experience as a person — beyond my work as a therapist — I pause, become quiet and allow myself the awareness of the presence of God. It is in that state, I commit to resolving whatever issue is at hand. Creativity, being alert, reaching out for help — in these ways I sooner or later find the path of wiser choice.

While pausing and thus reflecting, the ever-present loving Energy heightens. In that state, I give myself the responsibility, the self-accountability to resolve the dilemma currently at hand. Example: Dear Lord, In your presence I acknowledge that I need help to keep my eyes open for the paths of action that will help me actualize what I need to accomplish at this time.

That form of self-accountability is empowering. There is a sort of synergy, a partnership for the exercise of the loving teachings found in the Bible when seeking solutions to my dilemmas. It is a type of Energy sharing as well as a sort of team play. As such, I am available to work on and achieve good outcomes.

Self-responsibility type of mattering becomes central to resolution. Such an approach to accountability also frees me to broaden my cause to larger than the self. It transcends into the mattering of you, the mattering of others. That concept is the reason this book is dedicated to Joyce Morris, Shirley Anderson and Arnold Van Den Berg. They helped me to matter, each in their own way. Now I hope you find this book helpful in amplifying the fact that you too matter. Mattering is making quite the mind/body wellness impact upon me. I want to share that kind of energy with you.

Remember, when *you matter*, your life isn't the only one that gets better. It's every life you 'm a t t e r i n g l y' touch. So, helping your o w n cause wholesomely is helping humanity's cause. *Now that's heroic.*

Put the Air Mask on First: Actualizing Wellness Signals the Readiness to Parent

A major component in the act of parenting is mattering's exemplification. Children are a lot more likely to do as you do, not as you say. If you "practice what you preach" a child will more easily follow. Anyone who has worked in any kind of leadership role, for example as a schoolteacher, knows quality exemplification is key to quality follower-ship. If you enact what you ask of others, respectful follower-ship is more likely to happen. Children are sponges and, in a sense, copycats. When we show them the way to behave rather than preach to them, they are far more likely to follow in our footsteps.

What also needs to be understood is the fact that newborns, from the moment of sight, of visibility, are eying a parent intently.

Why? *Their survival depends on your attention, your attentiveness.*

Inherently, a child knows that is key to survival. That is why, when you have a second child, if the first one isn't secure with you yet, sibling rivalry erupts as the second demands your attention. This generally means the loss of some degree of security for the first-born child. That rivalry can definitely worsen as birth is given to the third, the fourth, the fifth. This rivalry is about supremacy, with victory going to the one who *seems* to gain the most attention. And yes, that rivalry is *primal*. It *is* about survival of the fittest. Knowledgeable parenting can avoid or lessen the potential for that pitfall.

When we are aware of this phenomenon, we can find ways to develop sibling teamwork; we can provide our children an anti-competitive environment. If not, the more competitive the need for attention, the greater the likelihood that at least one of the "rivals" will conclude, "I am a loser," "I am unlovable," "I don't deserve to be heard," "I don't deserve to be paid attention to" and/or "I am not good enough." Imagine how having a bunch of those identities must feel? Imagine the damage to the child, the misery plus the potential damage to the lives that individual's life touches.

Negative self-defining moments create a belief system that will actualize with unhappiness and produce less than desirable consequences until those beliefs are altered. *The definitions in those self-defining moments* of being a loser, unlovable, not good enough *dictate the behavior and the resulting emotions.*

Neural networks are formed to implement those beliefs' definitions. Consider the question: "Why do two people who have the same self-concept differ either somewhat or a lot in how they implement the self-concept belief?" Their <u>definitions differ</u> either slightly or majorly but can be altered.   Knowing that empowers change among siblings. That is what will affect relative closeness among them. Then from the beginning, children who also receive exemplification, instruction and positive reinforcing support in how to shift direction will get along better. And, if you are not able to do it on your own, and if there isn't a mind-body wellness center in your community, as there should be, we can be thankful there is a process like core healing: the shift out of a negative self-concept or belief into a positive. Core healing yourself can succeed in changing such beliefs to their positive opposites for those of you who wish to rewire the unfortunate beliefs imprinted in your mind-body. The shift may happen quickly or it may take time. Again, it's about direction not perfection. You will improve by not allowing any other of your negatives interfere. "I choose it as my right to be better, to get better, plus love me and others better".

Knowing this, it can be realized that out of sibling rivalry "losers" are made, not born. As exemplified here, it is simply the sad case of the child who gets the most attention wins. Or, the one born first wins. The twin who is born next does not. That child came in second. In other words, those who believe they are not attended to as much, or, come to think of themselves not just as losers, but additionally as a host of other related negatives are in trouble. What is saddest of all is witnessing a parent calling their child a loser and imprinting that painful identity directly.

Sibling rivalry unattended can create other negative identities: not being as smart as the other, not mattering (like the "other" seems to), being unworthy of love unlike the "other," and being "second" (not the culturally conceived comfort of being first). All can quite regrettably and unwittingly pass from generation to generation in most homes. Amorally, that child's brain enacts, amplifies, and gathers further and similar beliefs about self, such as: "I don't deserve to be heard, meaning understood, so what I say isn't even worth saying." Plus, there was that old — but not harmless — saying still ever present and governing in many, many adults: "You should be seen but not heard."

As a person, a parent, or a prospective parent, you are likely enacting one or more of these negatives yourself. It's not your parent's fault because, until now, they were ignorant of what you are currently learning. You, on the other hand, are herein being informed as to what to look for and change about yourself so your child(ren) will follow your lead. In Chapter Twelve you'll learn about other kinds of help for the damage your negatives may have caused you.

And, do remember to take care of you first. If you are going to be a parent, "put the mask on first." Get rid of and replace the key negatives with their positive opposites. Your brain has "neuroplasticity," which is a fancy word that means you can rewire your brain to actualize better self-concepts and beliefs. Then, you will be far more ready to parent due to better, though not necessarily perfect, exemplification. Your children will grow up healthier by virtue of your healthier example. But above all, please don't fall into the trap of demanding yourself to be a perfect parent.

Perfectionism is about not allowing yourself to matter unless you are perfect. That means you hardly, if ever, see yourself as good enough unless you are perfect. That's not just stressful but potentially insanity producing. At its zenith, at its worst, perfectionism is a killer. To some degree, almost all of us suffer as perfectionists, even though consciously we downplay it as a factor in our lives. That downplay is a grave error. Even graver is when we downplay it as a parent. If I have to be a perfect parent, the only way I can achieve that is by pressuring my child to be perfect. That's a disaster in the making.

To do a better job parenting, reparent yourself or get help from a core healer. Put the air mask on first before your child grows up suffering anoxia, being breathless even in some cases asthmatic. I'll never forget the client I treated for asthma. As a newborn, she wasn't able to breathe in enough love that left her gasping for it.

Physical problems of this or any other sort when presented for therapy later in life should always be checked hypno-analytically for metaphoric components. You'd be absolutely amazed at the psychogenic origins of illness that can easily be cured. Why hasn't this route been taken? I'm not the first to know the power of the mind for healing.

Regardless, as you invest yourself in healthy parenting with the help of what you are learning here, a positive result can be that you will be more able to selectively choose from among the pediatricians and quite critically the parenting guide books out there. The books pose questions about how many, if any, children to have and when to have them, what skills you need to demonstrate and teach, how to handle discipline — topics all so very critical to intentional versus happenstance parenting.

Parenting must become a readiness to quality parent issue. It cannot be governed by historic, enslaving, often religious sources of unrelenting baby making resulting from our normal sexual desire and/or ne ed for intimacy. When those ancient rules were established there was no way to envision, no way to imagine our eating and burning our way through our world's resources. There was no way to guess how a family barely surviving financially in today's world could possibly be a baby making factory and survive. To salvage our world, we need to think of baby making as a privilege, a decision carefully thought through.

It is that same common sense regarding responsible readiness that needs to be developed into a skill set for good parenting. Structured guidelines need communal agreement. Expectation clarification that insists upon *having the time and financial wherewithal* that would make quality parenting possible would be quite the blessing.

Moreover, taking the pressure off of unrealistic baby making will allow you to be free of the type of impatience that leads to mistake number one punitiveness. It is far better to help your child learn from the natural consequences of their mistakes as opposed to punitiveness.

Punitiveness is so damaging that it is one of the most critical issues to consider. Punitiveness arises very often from tiredness, fears of inadequacy, impatience and/or violent parenting that you yourself experienced as a parenting norm. Another tip, I would avoid any parenting guide book that uses the concept of punishment either overtly stated or implied. Being strict is different. Being strict and structured where necessary is appropriate. Just remember the shepherd's staff wasn't used to beat the sheep, it was used to guide their direction.

The Skills of Living an Easier Life More Worth Living

Not only at home but also in school, a whole range of skills need to be taught. These skills that include communication, logical thinking, thoughtfulness and ethics are *imperative to be learned*. Since parenting is the most important job in the world, our world should be supportive of wholesome readiness to parent in every way possible. Our elementary, middle and high schools should be teaching the necessary skills that will significantly reduce pain and suffering. But, what skills other than the few mentioned above ? Numerically listed below are 12 critical ones.

1. SOCIALIZATION.

Think of this as how we:
• Comfortably greet and chat with someone being met for the first time and subsequent times. It requires practice, especially for those whose parents aren't the greatest of models in doing that.

• "Pick up the ball," so to speak, after saying or doing something "dumb." We all say or do stupid things at times. This conversation recovery skill should extend to the development of wise self-talk, and the development of a sense of humor about certain types of fumbles. Something like: "Man, that coffee I just spilled is making an interesting path down the leg of my slacks," "Thank goodness I wasn't wearing shorts," or "Thank goodness I can go home for lunch so I can change my slacks before I have to be back at work." Or . . . "I think my boss is so competitive, he enjoys it when I fumble. It makes him look smarter than me in front of others."

Learning these ways of talking to yourself, of automatically getting into the solution, of using a sense of humor — all will serve you well.

• Speak in front of a group without fearing ridicule. When a child does a recitation in front of their classmates, if they fumble in some way and if their classmates haven't been pre-prepared to be supportive and so instead laugh and point, that child up front feels humiliated. In that moment of fear and humiliation reactive decisions are born like: "I fear public speaking," or "I'll likely make a dumb mistake and be laughed at."

There are techniques to make public speaking fun. One is learning how to fumble and pick up the ball and run with it. That is empowering. Learning such skills allows for promotion of what's important, what really matters in your presentation. It allows you to matter when, in an appropriate forum, you are needed to shine.

2. Confrontation (not confrontative) Skill Development

People generally fear confrontation. But, done constructively versus destructively, it is a precious skill to exercise. Constructive here is meant to suggest respectful and helpful in achieving better outcomes through clarification and co-creativity than by not confronting.

Confrontation, at its wisest exercise, eliminates the potential for festering. Instead, a potential is created for something better resulting from the clarification.

By each person coming from a place of wanting to understand and honor the other's point of view but with agreement that compliance with the other is not required, they have the potential for the most usefulness from such skill. Quality confrontation is not about overpowering the other. That's the work of bullies.

Overpowering type confrontation engenders defensiveness and retaliatory backlash. It eliminates the potential for co-creativity and beneficial outcome for both parties involved in the confrontation. A better understanding of the issue and the potential for a co-creative resolution get lost in the battle.

Confrontation is not about being a demolition derby. It's about resolving differences with others who matter as much as we do.

When learning to constructively confront someone in an effort to improve a situation or a relationship, *"lead with the feeling."* One feeling to be very careful of leading with is anger. As an example of a poor lead-in, cursing at someone, telling them how "damn dumb" they are, would be one. That means the possibility for resolution of difference is DOA.

It is extraordinarily important to understand, if you don't already, that *anger is a secondary emotion. Some stirred up <u>fear</u> within a person <u>is the immediate cause for the anger</u>.* Our society generally exemplifies skipping over the expression of one's fear and moving instead right into a negative energy release in the use of anger. An example is 'flipping the bird'.

Men, especially those raised with unrealistic, pain causing definitions of what being a man means, are more prone to doing this. Anger looks tough. Anger intimidates. Culturally, anger can convey power. You might hear somebody say: "Don't get *him* mad at you, or you'll be sorry." The actual underlying truth is: Don't make him scared because when he is, he becomes nasty, and can even be dangerous. Unfortunately for all concerned, this poor guy has been raised to play the King Kong role. That sucks the joy potential out of life not just for him but from those with whom he comes into contact.

Poor anger management generally results from lousy management imprints hardwired in the brain. To change such wiring, start practicing leading with the primary emotion, which is fear. For example:

It scared me when . . .

I became afraid for your life when you drank too much and drove home that way last night.

Again, fear is the primary emotion to its secondary anger not just sometimes but always. A person may not see the connection right away. Sometimes the fear is flavored with a sense of unfairness or injustice but then what is the fear that resides behind the anger of being treated unjustly, unfairly? It will happen again?

Earlier, an example was given as to how we learned to slide over fear and into an anger position. The example was when cut off unsafely and by surprise while driving. Perhaps without even realizing it, many of us have learned to believe that "flipping the bird" is a relief from the tension of a fear for one's safety. This reaction is an example of how our hard wiring works with such immediacy. It is an example of how our stored beliefs not our thoughts governed the reactive behavior with one's middle finger directly.

Much of the body's reaction to fear is situationally learned. The body at the speed of light is reactive and immediate. Depending on the stimulus creating the fear is how one reacts. It is situationally dependent.

When an anger situation is at hand in reaction to a fear, here's an example of a better way to communicate a challenging message. "When you said you need to take a break from parenting our troubled daughter that scared me. It's a challenge for both of us. Why don't we get help from our community wellness center or a licensed psychotherapist in private practice who specializes in family issues such as ours to help us better handle the situation together?"

This example for constructive confrontation can lead to a compassionate, loving outcome for all concerned. But both parents must be free to embrace such style of conflict resolution.

3. LEARNING THE LIFE SKILLS OF LOVING

These skills include:
- Empathy
- Compassion
- Attentiveness
- Reflective listening
- Thoughtfulness

- Harmless joking
- Romance and its appropriate setting
- Gentle/kind
- Encouragement of others' dreams and purposes in life
- Dependable
- Truthful
- Unconditionally accepting

4. MONEY MANAGEMENT

5. WHAT AND WHY BEING RESPONSIBLE IS SMART

6. LEARNING HOW TO FAIL WISELY

7. BEING SKILLED IN SELF-DEFENSE

8. REPLACING FEAR WITH THE CONCEPT OF I HAVE A CONCERN IN NEED OF A SOLUTION

9. BEING ADEPT AT TAKING ONE'S CONCERNS AND CREATING SOLUTIONS FOR THEM (STRATEGIC THINKING)

10. ASPIRING TO BE TRIM AND FIT, NOT SKINNY, NOT BIG AND STRONG OR FAT AND JOLLY. (THERE ARE SOLUTIONS TO TAKING HEALTHY CONTROL OVER YOUR EATING. CORE HEALING IS A KEY ONE.)

11. BALANCED LIVING BETWEEN WORK, FAMILY, CIVIC DUTIES AND A LIFE OF PLAYFULNESS AND SPONTANEITY. (C. Hammond)

12. LEARNING THE SKILL OF WISE DECISION-MAKING/LEADERSHIP: THE ABILITY TO ANTICIPATE CONSEQUENCES.

Notice, I didn't give explanation or pointers on all of the above. Some of those are found elsewhere in this book. Some, I am not knowledgeable enough to teach. You will find more authoritative experts on money management, self-defense and a balanced style. In terms of wise decision-making, I am only recently better at anticipating consequences for myself (but am great at it when Core Healing). The dean of girls in my high school unwittingly led me to believe I was "poor at anticipating consequences." I'm undoing that by replacing that belief with I am getting much better *at slowing down* to think through what the various types of consequences might be just as I am able to for my clients.

Again: It's about direction, not perfection.

❄

Part 2

CORE HEALING - FROM ILLNESS TO WELLNESS

6

Core Healing
TRUTH'S FREEDOM TRAIL

CORE HEALING IS A PROCESS. Early in the 1980s, I experienced this not as yet named, hypnotherapeutic process. It was awesome. The results were immediate and enduring beyond any talk psychotherapy I had ever personally experienced or witnessed. It gave me a way to implement the deeper passion behind my choice of profession: to ease pain and suffering in the world.

While I did not invent *any* of the techniques or the processes that I either experienced or subsequently learned, I am able to select and utilize the best from among them for enduring outcome. Together, those techniques are menus for both hypnoanalytic plus psychotherapeutic healing modalities that can be purposefully selected as need arises during a session.

The hypno-analytic investigative techniques are seeking relevant client memories and felt senses that surface while addressing each "why" question chosen for that day's session. Information I glean during this discovery phase lays the groundwork for the development of the healing phase.

I find it a relief that the core healing process allows for the fact that neither the client nor I are perfect. We just have to be determined to uncover the whole set of beliefs that exist in the constellation. That is doable. No crystal ball needed, just persistence.

It is rare that a client and I fail altogether. I've learned from experience a way to start with "talk therapy," which instructs the client how to assist in his or her own success.

It's also comforting for a client to know that the healing phase, which follows the discovery phase, can be flexed to address all five categories of any of their human, brain-body issues: behavioral, emotional, relational, physical, and/or spiritual.

The content of the discovery phase determines which of these categories need to be addressed for resolution. And each of those categories dictate the appropriate techniques selected by the therapist as the gears shift from discovery to healing phase in order to resolve the issues reflected in the "why" questions addressed. It's good to know that five to ten "why" questions can be resolved in one core healing session. Generally, a session lasts about two and a half hours.

Some of my favorites among the "old" healing techniques learned in graduate school and in seminars include:
• Cognitive Behavioral Therapy [Beck, 1976]
• Cognitive Reframing [in the manner of Happy Children by Dreikurs, 1972], [Grinder, 1981], [Riese, 1966] and [Milton Erickson, as reported by Rossi and Ryan, 1985]
• Love, Medicine and Miracles [Siegel, 1986]
• Direct Decision-Making Therapy [Greenwald, 1973]
• Transactional Analysis [Harris, 1969]
• Pivotal, the main type of "inner child work" I learned from my own therapist fifty years ago [Donald Tyrell: 1972 & 1977]

All of these influence my core healing work to this day though I am shifting my focus from being a psychotherapist to that of a teacher. Unfortunately, some of these greats are now out of fashion and not even taught anymore. They need to continue to be part of the current healing arts because aspects of their work remain powerfully effective.

Out of the loam of my history, the rich aspects of my graduate studies, my experience with the essence of this hypno-therapeutic process, my post-doctoral continuing education (especially through the American and Florida Societies of Clinical Hypnosis), and a profoundly well-timed and effective spiritual revelation — yes out of all these — the hypno-therapeutic process became my specialty in the mid-1980s. My clients christened it: "core healing."

The concept of psychotherapeutic "core" work wasn't in vogue then, as it is now. A couple of decades ago, when searching for a meaningful way to refer to this process, I turned to my clients for help. At the conclusion of the adventure of our work together, I would ask: "What would you say is different about what you experienced here in comparison to the other types of therapy and/or the medications that you experienced in the past?" Invariably, after thoughtful reflection, they responded, "This process healed me at my core."

I checked online. There was a spotty number using the adjective "core." So, thanks to my clients, the name "core healing" was chosen. And it was rightfully named. And now it turns out, it is even effective at the core of a person's cellular being. It is a comprehensive, mind-body, rapid and quite potentially complete healing in the five ways mentioned: behaviorally, emotionally, spiritually, relationally, and physically.

Following are two tips on entering this journey.

1. Engaging in the core healing process requires the selection of a licensed mental health professional well trained in the various ways to use hypnosis therapeutically. Ideally, that professional would themselves have experienced being '"core healed," as was I. Thus enabled, the "how" of more clearly seeing *my own* "within," *my own* revelations of self-discovery, honed my ability to seek the "within," the troublesome beliefs, of my clients.

2. A word of caution, which may just be me speaking. Do not choose a "certified hypnotist." Choose a licensed health professional certified as a *clinical* hypnotherapist. Why? My analogy is: Would you select a "state-approved surgeon" based upon his being trained for sixty hours in the different ways of using a scalpel? Or, would you want a physician who has done their residency in surgery?

Choosing to Look Under the Hood

Many people are afraid to "look under the hood," to go to their "within" and reveal their "true" selves. Their frightening assumption is that they have done something dark, something evil as a child that they don't remember and that is causing them to behave "wrongly," unhealthfully, hurtfully or unhappily.

However, the truths behind *everyone's* problems, the hundreds upon hundreds I have worked with . . .no matter how haunting and with *no* exception, the truth behind their problems is not their fault. Let me repeat that because it goes against what we have all been taught.

The following concept cannot be emphasized enough:

> People are not at fault for what they think, feel, or do because <u>they have no choice</u>, no free will, no ability to do other than <u>what their relevant beliefs allow</u>, either for better or for worse.

Until such time that beliefs as an individual's truths are altered for the better in a heightened awareness state and that these changed beliefs support the thought-based, better judgment choices desired, a person is trapped in the governance of the negative beliefs that unfortunately were imprinted in their brain-bodies.

Ridding a person from the fear of being irrevocably at fault better allows for being forgiving, most especially of self. Forgiving, as defined here, means letting go of pain and anger. That definition is incredibly important to thorough healing.

With core healing's hypno-analytic truth-seeking, what invariably emerges and demonstrates is what was *done to* the person. It shows the harmful actions that have robbed them of decent, wise, and caring choices. It shows the reasons why unwholesome identities formed. Identities that are mean and hateful of self and others are developed in the child either wittingly or unwittingly but not by them *originally*. The foundation for a child adopting ugly beliefs and self-concepts, has to have been laid. These understandings taught during the "talk therapy" prep time can aid in opening the door to welcoming therapeutic forgiveness, the release of shame and guilt in the healing phase.

Depending on the foundation laid, the reactive decisions of a child or teenager about themselves become their actualizing identities. These can enhance their goodness or cultivate "evil" conduct. It does not resemble the myths about Zeus stuffing all manner of evil within their Pandora's "box." Nor is the evil created through the temptation and invitation of an invented devil. Such myths, throughout history are but imaginative stories offering some way to understand threatening, ugly behavioral mysteries. Unfortunately, these forces have been used to terrorize and manipulate.

All manner of evil behavior — behavior that is abusive, conniving, self-serving and/or sabotaging, racist, cruel, even murderous —

are majorly a result of people lacking such pivotal identity as, "I am a kind, caring person who does what is ethically right."

Moreover, empathy for the ethically impoverished is more likely absent altogether. Such a person is an inherent "loser." Their familial, culturally cultivated untrue, unwholesome beliefs, yes, the

u gly beliefs cause the rot in their beings. Their rot becomes
u their next generation's rot. (These plus other such ideas are listed in the aptly entitled glossary: Illness Developing Beliefs.)

The illness producing list is long. Over the past several years, other forms of imprinting have added to the current illness list due to the dystopic, dark, gruesome, terrorizing, sociopathic behavior witnessed in movies, games, dark web sites, tabloid news, all wreaking havoc.

Vividly blasted, scary images in so many forms of gaming and movies home grown or otherwise imprint into a person's psyche. Their nightmarish imprints are horrific and causal of evil, especially in the minds of those with welcoming belief constellations. They offer depressing, anxiety provoking and even quite dangerous imprints.

Arriving at this point in my book, I hope, I pray, you do what I advise my clients. While what you are doing is not your fault, it is your responsibility to improve yourself so as to live at peace within, share that peace with others, and restore peace on Earth. As the song goes: "And, let it begin with me." (See the Wellness glossary.)

We don't need to be afraid of this responsibility. When we are praised even if just from ourselves, realize that we are admired for learning from our failures and mistakes, allowing us to move forward as a result. After all, that's what true gold medalists do. They even take pictures of their mistakes to learn from them.

When such learning is labeled "smart," is praised for the truth-seeking required, and the best practices chosen for correction, it creates the freedom for constructive reaction for improvement.

Wiser alternatives then become the agenda. In other words, if mistakes are taken as learning opportunities instead of punitive triggers, we remove the fear of taking responsibility.

So, from seeking one's inner truths that allow for alternative transplants for the negative self-concepts and beliefs so that better ones are enacted, the reward is huge. It's your ever increasing freedom to be calm and at peace. Hooray for looking under the hood.

The Goals for Core Healing

The goals for core healing include the freedom to:

- Be free to matter equally.
- Live purposefully / lovingly.
- Be a gentle 're-parenter' of oneself by choosing and actualizing healthy, wellness ways of life. (See Glossary A)

- Make better choices unembarrassed to use one's failures to make wiser choices, including of a marital sort.
- Love wisely and well, fostering wholesome relationships and — where appropriate — passionate, ever romantically thoughtful ones.
- Foster sibling teamwork.
- Work toward the common good.
- Be active community decision-makers.
- Be successful without <u>having to live stress-filled lives</u>.
- Have fun. Live a balanced, wellness-oriented life.
- Be attentive.
- Be compassionate and caring of self, as well as others.
- Connect into the loving Energy legacy.
- Enjoy being who you are, basically and fundamentally good.
- Find the joy in being continuously well informed versus defensively ignorant.
  (Following this list is a client's story about her core healing journey increasing her wellness oriented capacity.)

This is that story of one woman's physical healing. It is not a "cure" story but an enduring improvement story in the client's own words written from her core healing experience four years ago. Notice her ability to have greater self-awareness.

When diagnosed with Parkinson's, I thought I was on an impending journey down a slippery slope. The following is what I believe to be a testament to core healing with Dr. Glasser, though rarely do I *focus on having Parkinson's disease.* I just don't think about it.

My MD is amazed at how well I am doing. And, it's only on the rare occasion when someone brings up the subject of me having PD, do I tend to become symptomatic. It's as if they have called the disease to come out, come out, wherever you are. I then present with a slight tremor in my left hand and perhaps, but not always, a slight tremor in my left leg.

Oh, and what about this? Prior to every doctor's appointment, I'm answering twenty-five or so questions related to whether I am experiencing this or that symptom or having this or that difficulty, once again being reminded that I have PD, and so wouldn't you think I would start tremoring? But I don't. I never do. I almost feel guilty that I can't answer in the affirmative to any of the questions relating to "worsening symptoms" or "difficulties" as asked on the questionnaire. Each time I complete this exercise, I gather the doctor will think I'm in denial or am lying, of which neither is the case! Core healing won't allow me to give in to getting worse. But remember, I don't consciously think about it. It just happens.

Carrying on with daily activities just as I had done before the disease is the norm in my world. There exist no boundaries as to what I am capable of accomplishing with regard to anything I do, especially physical labor. Aside from being more observant and careful which comes not only with age but with having PD, I still climb ladders to wash my windows because I'm too cheap to hire someone. I still do my own housework because no one is as meticulous and fussy as I. I still take care of my four dogs. I still enjoy each day God has given me. My life has not changed one bit. Frankly, I forget I have PD. I don't act like I do and certainly NEVER give it an opportunity to control me to the point I become symptomatic except for the aforementioned example. I feel that's pretty remarkable.

Yes, I do take medication three times a day, one with a known side effect of wearing off before the next dosage. The good news is I don't experience that either. But why? There's something in my brain that won't allow it. There's something in my brain that's blocking the symptoms from manifesting and that something replaced what could have been opened floodgates if not for my core healing journey.

Thankfully, I have not developed any other symptoms nor have they worsened. Sadly though, I know others, younger and older than I, who have undergone many procedures i.e. deep brain stimulation or who have been given a bevy of medications in an attempt to control the worsening symptoms but yet who are now more debilitated than before to the extent of having become dependent on others because they allowed the disease to overtake their mind. They seem to have chosen being consumed with the disease and have convinced themselves, "I have Parkinson's and I'm supposed to be this way." The disease rules their mind and so if they believe they are incapacitated, then they are. If they believe they are incapable of doing things, then they can't. My subconscious on the other hand has taken control of my "here and now" in a good way so that my PD rarely crosses my mind thereby preventing it from rearing its ugly head.

So, to answer your question Dr. Glasser, my core healing work with you ended up being a HUGE partner in my Parkinson's disease journey. I define core healing as a complementary therapy that I am grateful for but not presently aware of...which is the way it should be!

This gal was a delight to work with and, as a retiree, is now working five days a week as a volunteer. While "cheap" in spending money by washing her own house's windows, she is not cheap with her time helping others. She knows she matters.

As One Who Matters, You May Seek Your Path to.....

"Why Are You Here?"

Consider the following words by Head Coach Rhett Power at Power Coaching and Consulting.

Have you discovered your *purpose* — why you're here, what you're meant to do? How do you know when you have found your purpose? And why do you need to find it?

Because it's where you find fulfillment and satisfaction. It's what gets you out of bed in the morning and makes time fly. "Your purpose may be to be an incredible parent, teacher, or nurse, or to bring joy to people through the arts," writes well-being author James McWhinney. "Your purpose is highly important regardless of the size or scale of reach – every single person has an important role to play."

Some people seem to be born knowing what brings them joy and meaning. Most of us, though, need help figuring it out for ourselves. Here are five questions to get started:

1. *What makes me feel happy and alive?*

Your purpose is often related to what you love to do. It might — or might not — be connected to your career. Or you might find it while volunteering or in your favorite hobby. Think about what you most look forward to and consider how you can expand those activities into more of your life.

2. What am I good at?

Don't be so humble. We all have talents and skills — what are yours? You might have the ability to build things, the patience to be a mentor, or the vision of a leader. You'll find more success in using natural strengths than in trying to get rid of your self-perceived weaknesses.

3. If income didn't matter, what would I be doing?

This question often leads directly to the discovery of your purpose. The answer can point you in the direction of your true happiness. Maybe you work in a large corporation but dream of being an entrepreneur. Don't let yourself get stuck; start taking small steps to reach your goal.

4. How can I add greater value to the world?

When you take time to become self-aware, you can see where to use your knowledge and skills. You might be passionate about helping the elderly, building a new playground for the neighborhood, or changing laws in your city. Each of us has unique interests that can be used to make the world a better place.

5. What will be my legacy?

Your purpose in life can affect how you will be remembered; it's an opportunity to leave your mark on the world. Ask yourself how you can make a positive difference in the lives of others.

When you begin to consider your purpose, you are on your way to the happiness and enthusiasm that will enrich your life and the lives of others. Your natural focus will drive you to reach your goals — and you will become successful, on your own terms. Why not start today?

❄

The Purpose of Life

Learning to Live Lovingly, Joyfully, Wisely and Well.

"When you are inspired by some great purpose, some extraordinary project, all your thoughts break their bonds: Your mind transcends limitations, your consciousness expands in every direction, and you find yourself in a new, great and wonderful world. Dormant forces, faculties and talents become alive, and you discover yourself to be a greater person by far than you ever dreamed yourself to be."
~Patanjali

Because Each and Every One of You Were Born to Matter

Quote provided by: Arnold Van Den Berg

7

Unearthing Trauma's Rot

The Degrees of PTSD: We All Suffer Post Traumatic Stress

IT'S NOT JUST the veterans who suffer so hugely from the traumas of the war zone. There are war zones in our homes between parents and siblings; among races and religions; in our classrooms; between lovers; within our communities; and on the internet.

We are seeing the enslaving, cruel, and murderous abuse of women and children, warring between competing despots of various countries. In our own nation, we see internal warring factions. All of these things leave their varying traumatic imprints, their potentially, enduringly hurtful, crippling and/or suicide-fostering outcomes.

But before clarifying what Core Healing has taught me about traumatic effects and resolution, we need to be on the same page regarding what is meant by PTSD, or post-traumatic stress disorder.

Post-traumatic stress disorder, now often referred to as a reaction, occurs at any age. Following here are some examples of it surfacing. They include:

- A surprise event can wound the brain-body (either physically like a gunshot to the shoulder or mentally like finding one's spouse in bed with someone else).
- We repetitively experience emotional and/or physical wounding (like verbal and/or physical abuse).
- A terrifying event occurs like watching your soldier buddies blown to bits or listening to your mother threatening suicide when you are little.
- One is surprised as in when an event occurs without warning.
- We experience prolonged terrorizing acts such as random beatings and torture.
- Our lives are perceived as threatened (in utero, infancy, childhood, adulthood).

The nature of the negative reactive decision [NRD] in response to a trauma will be predictive of the degree of psychic consequence. Most often, the NRDs are subconsciously, quite logically and instantaneously determined by the computer brain-body based on another of that person's NRDs. That is why a person does not consciously know why they are having the degree of reaction experienced.

So, how would one measure the size, the intensity of the post-traumatic stress reaction due to these NRDs? Obviously, it would be based upon the degree of trauma ranging from depression in the form of occasional sadness to suicide ideation or enactment, and from anxiety experienced as monthly nightmares to drinking uncontrollably.

The Negative Brain-Body Imprints: Graphic and Verbal

When a post-traumatic stress event occurs, there are both graphic and verbal imprints into the brain-body, which may or may not be consciously remembered. It seems that graphic memories beyond the age of about eight are more readily remembered. Generally, the verbal imprints as negative reactive decisions, while not consciously remembered, are not forgotten either. They are hard-wired into the neural network of the various parts of the brain.

TO RECAP:

Question: What do people do so swiftly that they don't consciously remember?
Answer: Their speed-of-light, computer brain generates self-concepts and beliefs based upon the self-concepts and beliefs already held.
Example: I'm not smart enough.
Resulting in a new self-concept: I'll never get it right.

Question: How does the event affect the brain-body?
Answer A: By creating new neural connections with which to implement the additional belief.
Bodily systems implement relevant beliefs reactively. They are at the service of the belief software's programming.
Answer B: By creating a graphic imprint of the PTSD event that may or may not be consciously remembered.
And, Answer C: By developing a related biological marker associated with the event that is imprinted as well.

Question: How and why do different individuals experiencing the same potentially traumatic circumstance, experience effects that differ in magnitude or have no negative effect at all?
Answer: It depends on pre-existing self-concepts and beliefs. For example, how would a person with the self-concept: "I am resilient" respond differently from one who believes "I am weak" or "I am always the one at fault".

Question: How young does a human being begin experiencing effects from trauma?

Answer: In utero.

Traumas can happen in utero, during birthing, and anytime there-after. The negative, but also positive reactive decisions, NRDs and PRDs, develop at the speed of light. They imprint into the brain. They create a neural network for implementation as a relevant situation arises. Below are some actual examples of negative self-concept development situations.

Question: Why, when anxious, do I smoke?

An *answer under hypnosis:* "I felt frantic. I had no way to throw up from the dizziness and nausea of my mother smoking. I had to get used to it to calm down." (An in utero felt sense.)

Another *answer under hypnosis*: "My grandfather gave me my first cigarette when we went fishing. We used to smoke together when I was a boy. It made me feel like a grown man, comforted and safe."

Question: Why have I gotten headaches all my life? An answer under hypnosis: "When the doctor was delivering me, his hands were on either side of my head, twisting it while assisting my delivery as I was coming down the birth canal."

(She got headaches whenever something was a "pain in the neck.")

Question: Why did I get testicular cancer?
An answer under hypnosis: "At age 2....I wanted to disappear from feeling invisible and trapped." (Initial Sensitizing Event)
The cancer erupted due to subsequent events. The client was worried about effects on his children due to an ugly divorce (of feeling trapped in marriage for decades). **NRD:** *"I am to be punished with cancer because it is something I can't get rid of"......leaving the guy feeling like he did at age 2 = stuck in a scared to death situation you can't get out of.*

Question (common for soldiers): *Why am I so depressed, even suicidal? Perceptions:*
• I was the <u>coward</u>. It should have been me getting my leg blown off.
• It was <u>my fault</u>. I *should have,* or somehow, I *could have* done something to prevent it. (<u>Never being good enough</u>, even though he/she tried.)
• <u>I was the one who deserved to die</u>, not those guys.
• <u>I deserve to be punished</u> for not saving my buddy.

These all are examples of the types of negative reactive decisions (NRDs) made in immediate reaction to such trauma. Instantaneously, they become identities that form as self-concepts and beliefs to be implemented amorally by the mind-body without any sense of right or wrong, wise or harmful, or degree of consequence. The veteran's identity "I deserve to die" generates anxiety because it "goes against the [genetic] grain." I deserve to die as an identity belief, potentiates suicidal behavior, let alone being anxiety producing and likely to be carried out. Why? Because, "it should have been me who died."In a sense, how traumatizing the event and its imprint are, depends on already held NRDs. The degree of the problems the NRDs create can generate still further issues and sometimes make existing ones worse.

In summary, how does committing suicide compare to being a smoker or a person with headaches? How does it compare to getting cancer? All are "bad" outcomes based upon the developed NRDs with their traumatizing imprints. Their consequences can be judged as to their degree of harm to self and others. To see a visualization of this concept, note the gradually shrinking sizes of the letters below.

PTSD to PTSD **to** PTSD|

The Powerful and Painful Results of Traumatic Events

In and of themselves, traumatic events are painful. They result in psychic and/or physical injury of varying degrees of intensity and consequence, emotionally, behaviorally, physically, spiritually, and relationally. The degree of pain and suffering will be determined by both our NRDs and our PRDs (positive reactive decisions). The pain can be minimized by the PRDs or become maximal due to the NRDs. Healing can be sped up or slowed down. At worst, the pain and suffering can be so unbearable that a drastic escape, as in suicide and sometimes even murder, can seem the only "way out."

This whole issue of degree of pain and suffering depends upon a simple binary issue. Are more illness or more wellness beliefs governing an individual's life?

Based upon what you have learned here, the only person who would knowingly perpetuate illness is a very ill, irresponsible, uncaring person who assumes the "only I and mine matter" pattern of life. I hold out little hope for such pathetic lost souls.

THE REST of us can choose to live wellness self-concepts and beliefs. We can choose to matter equally and increasingly kindly. We can improve and invest ourselves in a world worth inheriting.

Our children are very scared with our poor stewardship. As well they should be. Most of us, without realizing it, have allowed ourselves to be escorted into the darkness of despotic times.

Either we become team salvation or we'll perish with the apocalypse we have created. Don't blame God if the most of us appoint others the tasks of wellness we should be incorporating and assisting with ourselves.

And, what should we do now that we know all this? Well, if we develop children with a fortress of positive self-concepts and beliefs, that is a great beginning. But, it does not mean that when a traumatic event occurs, they will experience zero pain or zero depression or zero anxiety. The perfect parent, the perfect environment doesn't exist. So, some negatives will imprint.

On the other hand, the PRDs minimize the reaction. Children, when raised well equipped, grow up increasingly immunized belief-wise, knowledge-wise and skill-wise.

Example: What have you been taught about how long and how intensely you are to grieve the loss of a spouse? How does that definition compare with the loss of a child? Or, of a grandparent? You will suffer to the degree you have been taught by example, culturally, and/or religiously as to what it means to "grieve" in each case.

Pain and suffering reduction management in this example requires rethinking. In other words, the process of recovering from a loss relates to the exercise and the use of best judgment, along with a solution orientation. One way to go about this process is asking yourself a question like this: What would my child, who loved me dearly want me to know as he died of cancer? What would my child want for me? What might our child wish we *believed* so that we didn't emotionally and physically fall apart suffering his physical loss?

I remember working with a woman of Italian heritage who was the first of her family to be born in the United States. She was still grieving the loss of her father after six years. The pain was intense enough that she couldn't even visit his grave site to seek comfort, pay her respects and offer her undying gratitude.

Under hypnosis, I asked her, "How do women in Italy grieve?"

She replied, "When the first family member dies, you wear black for a while. When the second family member dies, you wear black longer, and when the third one dies, you wear black for the rest of your life." They grieve their whole lives.

Then I asked her, "How do men in Italy grieve?"

She replied: "Oh, they weep and cry too. They beat their chests."

And I asked: "And, for how long?"

Her answer: "The men are done grieving in three weeks and go on with their lives."

So, I ask you readers, what would be the "cure" or at least the antidote to reduce suffering? What identity was she better off with when it comes to grieving?

PTSDs Are Curable

No matter the size of the PTSD, it is easier for the clinical hypnotherapist to rectify negative behaviors once a client learns their whole history of relevant truths leading up to the devastating NRD that was produced during the trauma event. The actual source of fault lies elsewhere. It lies in that person's enculturation, their upbringing, their definition for being a man (or a woman), in other words, in prior life events over which they had no control.

When the traumatic event is rationally and cognitively reframed in the healing phase of core work, where brain rewiring is doable, PTSD can be much more readily cured. My experience isn't just with everyday folks with PTSD but also covers my work with a large number of veterans as well.

Better Yet, PTSDs Are Preventable (or at least minimizable)

The flip side of negative reactive decisions are positive reactive decisions. The more PRDs we develop along the path of life, instantly, the easier it is to better react, to throw off the potential of negative effects from traumatic events. Those events clearly do happen. For that reason, we can't live in a society that so burdens us with financial pressures that we are too tired or too undereducated to make our lives easier and healthier by learning the skills necessary. Stop PTSD before it happens by building your fortress PRDs defining who you are as a humane individual.

Remember those educated better than us are not our enemies. Our enemy is our own ignorance. No, not me, not you, not any of us "know it all." But we can sure fill in the needed gaps. You'll recall the ideas in Chapter Six as to how to go about it. Filling these gaps is not a luxury. It is a necessity. Otherwise, illness in all its forms will continue to metastasize.

So, how about this as a motto:

Live Better Beliefs: Suffer Less; Enjoy Life More.

Maybe you have a better motto that will foster your well being. Use it. Imprint it. Become it. Illness can disappear and post traumatic stress reactions will be framed / imprinted better and grief reactions diminish or disappear.

✳

8

Pruning, Weeding, Nurturing
THE HEALING NEEDED AT CORE

As DISCUSSED EARLIER, most foundational "weed seed" negative self-concepts and beliefs are in place by the age of six. Some research suggests eighty percent of negative imprints have happened by then. What precise statistic actually applies? It remains to be determined. Research at neighborhood wellness centers could be conducted on this issue.

Be that as it may, you'll remember earlier in this book my thoughts on the way a child leans into the use of the word "why." This issue is being brought up again here in order to emphasize the point that so many of our *negative* self-concepts and beliefs begin in the simplistic language of a child. Examples include: I am fat. I am stupid. I am bad. I am evil. I am ugly. Punishment helps make things better. I don't like being punished. I am scared to be punished like that again. I am not lovable. I am not safe. Well, I guess I just don't matter.

As a therapist, the issue of "in the language of a child" emerged as an awareness since writing my last book about core healing published in 2007. Understanding that concept as a hypno-analyst/hypno-therapeutic healer improved my truth seeking investigative abilities and consequently improved outcomes on a client's behalf.

The more truths found in the form of developmentally early NRDs (negative reactive decisions) and then replaced with PRDs (positive reactive decisions), the more thorough one's self-empowerment, the more internal calm and the more self-confident an individual becomes. Clients love how that feels. Who among us wouldn't?

So, utilizing the knowledge about "in the language of a child," the core healing journey using hypnosis considerably broadens the scope for thorough resolution. On the other hand, when adults engage in talk therapy and attempt that same therapeutic outcome, while not necessarily fruitless, it is costly in terms of the years and years of precious time invested working toward a resolution. Co-pays, gasoline, the value of one's time, the cost of drugs both 'street' and/or prescribed, the cost of continued depressive and anxiety effects on not just self but loved ones, can be steep.

It is important to pause here and also consider the fact that two adults working in a talk therapy format conduct their discussion in their language as adults and not that of the client's injured or misguided child self. Moreover, a person's *sub conscious* recollections when engaged in talk therapy often are not available to discuss. The opportunity to go back to relevant memories and the NRDs attached to them is lost without the tool of hypnosis (which meditation is a form of) — particularly those events experienced before the age of six.

Talk therapy discussion of issues often is not even able to surface relevant NRD events from adulthood that need "fixing". They were subconsciously derived in a traumatic event even as recently as a month ago. (That's where I especially feel sorry for 'war' veterans including those on the front lines of the Corona virus war.)

Being able to have full range access to relevant memories whether in the language of a child or that of an adult requires the heightened awareness state that both hypnosis and meditation provides. No matter when the traumatic event occurred, it may have been formulated either in the language of the child self or the adult self. Unsurfaced, however, it cannot be resolved.

When my last book about core healing was published, I always suggested that clients address the following question notably in the language of an adult: "Why do I believe I deserve to be abandoned"? Abandonment? What? That's not in the vocabulary of a child. I didn't use that word myself until my mid-thirties.

Would we agree the abandonment question is not in the language of the child? Yes. Do most clients place it on their wish list of "why" questions to resolve? No. But some do. Regardless, as an issue, it still earns a prominent place in the mind of this therapist when working with each client. Its ramifications are huge.

As a sprawling outgrowth of a weed seed, the belief that "I deserve to be abandoned, meaning left alone, having no one there for me and most especially not even God," generates the *potential* for even further depression and anxiety as well as suicide. It produces beliefs like: "I am a loner," "I am unlovable," "I am bad," "I deserve to be punished," "I no longer deserve God's comfort or presence in my life" (the abandonment of self from God), "I deserve to die," or, "Since I can't handle it anymore, I'll go crazy" (a subconsciously concocted escape to a mental institution or a get-away-from-it-all holiday where "someone else will take care of me.") The latter two are forms of self-abandonment. Are they consciously thought through in those terms and consequences? Not typically.

When I worked at a psychiatric hospital, I had a Caucasian man as a client who was diagnosed as chronically depressed. He was really good at it. He was at least partially aware that he was acting depressed for what is called "secondary gain." Diagnosed as chronically depressed, he was placed on disability. Since there was no other means of taking care of his family he figured disability income was it.

Very often, our society robs people of opportunity to civilly survive. We abandon them to survive anyway they can. Then, we blame those who are in desperation taking such measures to survive at taxpayer expense. (As an inner city school principal, I watched that predicament play out there too. *It's our fault when everyone isn't raised to matter with equal opportunity to thrive*, and then we blame them for criminal or quasi-criminal results. We are at fault, not them. We created their ghettos. We 'redlined' them.)

Those negatives regarding abandonment do indeed need to be changed. But to be clear, from where in the language of the child did those weeds regarding abandonment begin? Answer: From the logical primal fear of being left alone. Example: An abandoned infant left in a dumpster in the middle of winter will die because of being left alone there. The terror of the predicament is imprinted even though the infant has no language with which to talk about it. Under hypnosis, a client can describe those felt senses if such a memory as that memory comes up relevant to one of their "why" questions.

Let's say that a child, thus abandoned, was rescued by a passerby. Out of that trauma, the fear of death, being "deathly afraid" of being left alone could certainly become a negative self-concept one that is more than just: "I fear being alone." It might be more like: "I freak out when alone."

Then, that weed-seed root grows deeper as the fear of being alone heightens. It begins to pervade one's being with subsequent reinforcing events like a babysitter leaving the child alone at age three because she didn't feel well and had to hurry home. Yes, the babysitter finally called the little one's parents and they came right home. However, there was that interim period of abandonment and endangerment.

The child didn't die. But the fear was broadening with a belief like: "I can't trust anyone to look out for me." Thus, the weed's sprawl reached out, developing even more relevant NRDs. Together, they become a whole bunch of related NRDs I call a constellation. The root's tendrils sprouted, strengthening the root's hold. The weeds' tentacles grew broader. Or, in other words, the person's constellation of negatives strengthened its grip and expanded with the additional negative self-concepts and beliefs. They began adding up as enacted. Enacted, they increased the person's poor behavior and misery.

Additional and related negative beliefs became further outgrowths. The fear of being alone constellation continued to increase based upon related events like the keen disappointment of a best friend not showing up to hang out as planned and not even calling or texting to give her a heads-up. Then, her first boyfriend dumps her for a prettier girl leaving her with a reinforced identity "well, I guess I'm somehow not enough to ever have a boyfriend." And even worse yet, the consciously and subconsciously derived NRDs helped generate and support her decision: "I'll join the vaping group; that way I'll have friends."

Now, what is beginning to be "made to happen" is not just happening incidentally. NRDs are growing her constellation into how to handle avoiding the pain and terror of being alone, the pain of abandonment. She is abandoning herself by vaping, a potential escape from life and the terrifying pain of the growing fear of aloneness and being unlovable.

A tyrant weed seed (the fear of being alone) sprawled over time. It grew its own set of NRDs into a constellation over time. It begins choking the lawn's (her life's) healthy growth. That fear becomes the broader, more dangerous self-concept: "I must deserve to be abandoned." It is in the language of the adult now drawing that conclusion.

Resolution is sped up understanding this language shift.

As the constellation grew over time in this way, so did the pain and suffering that the individual unwittingly would cause themselves and others. Their brain-body implemented damaging beliefs at every relevant turn of events.

- I fear being alone.
- I will die if left alone.
- I can't trust anyone to look out for me.

What would being married to someone like that become as they operationalize those beliefs? And, that's assuming she had a compelling belief to get married in the first place like: I'll have a child and he/she will be dependent on me. My child will be obligated to take care of me, be there for me when I am old. In this fashion, the NRDs weed seeds' sprawl is being evidenced in one's observable, self-defeating and harmful to self and to other behavior. That child will pay the price of misery along with its mom.

Consequently, it becomes easy to imagine how the young woman's pain and suffering was self-generating and growing more intense as her implementation of the expanding constellation resulted in increasing fear (anxiety), an increasing sense of being out of control (key factor in depression), an increasing anger with self (a major factor in the evidencing of depression) due to the inability to self-correct. Without the truth and the whole truth as to her constellation of misery beliefs her hope for swift freedom from anxiety and depression were next to nil. Without core healing, she would have to resort to neurofeedback, years of meditation practice, medication and/or talk therapy.

Is it fair then to ask: Was the suffering's consequence a matter of free will? No. Unless uncovered, unless enlightened, the woman couldn't possibly know all this self-identity development. And, therefore, in adult-with-adult talk therapy, there was no way to resolve the potential for all of its consequences. And not with therapist centered EMDR either unless the therapist gets lucky with their professional experience = good guessing at times.

With therapeutic failure, the sprawling intensification of the fear of being alone reaches out ever further. Then, when a professional can't even "fix" the woman, not by drug, not by earnest cognitive reframing, not even through some form of the seven types of meditative training, and not by other means, now the weed's sprawl reaches out further with the new belief in the language of the adult, "I am not fixable" or "I can't be cured" or "I am a lost cause," etc. Such progression brings increasing suffering and potentially suicide's ideation closer to reality.

The outgrowth emotional consequences over time intensify as the constellation grows. It's like a negative, emotion draining, wellness draining malignancy. The next chapter about anxiety and depression will further expand your understanding. They are the consequence of life events that are mismanaged, scary, unhappy, and yet, just so ordinary as to not even be questioned as sources to NRDs whether in the language of a child, a teen, an adult and yes even in the language of 'old folks'.

The Top Ten Universal Negative Self-Concepts and Beliefs in Need of Weeding and Better Yet Prevention

1. "I don't matter." (Or, only I and 'mine' matter".)
2. "I am bad." (Or worse, evil!)
3. "I am not good enough." (I am inadequate.)
4. "I must be perfect." (Or, I'll deserve to be punished or be abandoned and not able to survive independently.)
5. "I am dependent." (Becoming an adult child!)
6. "I fear being responsible."
7. "I deserve to be punished." Vengeance to self *and* with others is just. (It isn't. It is just inhumanely destructive.)
8. "I am unlovable."
9. "I am worthless." (a loser, a failure)
10. "I fear being alone." (I don't belong as who I am.)

For Contrast: Example of Positive Belief Constellation's Growth

When referring to a positive seed planted in one's brain-body (a positive identity imprint), I use the word "acorn." It is simply meant as a contrast to the notion of "weed" seed. Even though I'm not a metaphor expert, the comparison is only meant to serve for the purposes of initial contrast clarification.

To clarify, I am going to speak from my own history, my own experience. It helps to understand the concept by thinking of the acorn seed as part of a wholesome constellation's development from the 'get-go' of one's existence. (As a Core Healer, I weed out the negatives and then plant acorns [PRDs] to govern and grow in their stead.)

Usually, when sharing my personal history, it gets around to talking about my dad and his impact upon me. It was profound in many ways.

But, in the following example, it seems most appropriate to highlight a critical and impacting, wonderful acorn seed my mom planted: the idea that *being gentle is admirable*. (Being gentle should not just be copied as loving conduct but contextualized with the humbleness of her style whenever implanted.)

That imprint came about when I was in high school and the acorn seed of being a caring person allowed me to admire and appreciate what she *did*, not said, just simply, lovingly did. It was by *virtue* of a humble deed, an example she set. From it, I drew the highlighted conclusion in the previous paragraph. In other words, the lesson was not relayed with her words. She enacted, she exemplified that concept, which is the most powerful teacher of all. It conveys authenticity and the implicit message: This is its manner. This is *how* to do it.

Neither my mom nor I have been perfect models of that imprint. Regardless, for me over the years, it has grown in healthful, admirable, wonderful ways. A marvelous constellation of supportive beliefs grew from that acorn seed. They enhanced my behavioral and emotional existence. My style became more help-ful, more humane as a result.

Here's that acorn seed's impact within the context of its develop-ment. This is the constellation of two important additional PRDs fostered. They are presented following the order in which they developed.

• Growing up, I had learned how to react under certain circum-stances with ugly anger. On one particular occasion, I humiliated myself acting that way. That feeling of being intensely ashamed caused reflection as to what to do about it. So, I decided to replace the identity of doing ugly anger with being *gentle* instead. My reasoning: Being a thoroughly gentle person makes doing ugly anger impossible.

Regrettably, I haven't always been able to live that commitment, but I do get better at it. The motto of self encouragement that I created and enjoy sharing with others helps: It's about direction not perfection. Then too, there's a bonus. I enjoy witnessing these changes for the better while I live as a gentle woman. My caring identity, which was developed at age four, swells with pride when I succeed with even small successes. It becomes self reinforcing to do my best with it.

• Becoming among "the meek," the gentle *and* the *kind*, became an outgrowth of my embarking on a journey toward gentility. I was pretty ignorant as to the concept of kindness. I could recognize it in others. I could recognize caring conduct of my own but kindness seemed foreign.

Nonetheless, I did so admire kind people; it became an intense focus for learning and practicing the ways of being kind. It became a solid commitment I have never regretted.

The intensity of the commitment grew. I deeply wanted to be kind throughout every fiber of my being, in every cell of my body. I wanted it to shine out of me. That's how much I admired that quality when I witnessed it in others because along the way, I studied those who acted inherently kind. I liked how safe I felt with such people. And so, I wanted to emulate, to imitate until their style became my way of being, albeit, I am still improving. Regardless, such commitment has helped by enabling me to serve my clients better. I wanted for them what I was experiencing as a healthfully delicious way of life.

Serenity and wellness are more fully derived from being among the meek. That is the path for connectivity because being among the meek is the essence of our design. To better understand the inherent nature of this in us all, I want to further follow Yale and Harvard universities' studies on infants' meek response style *tendency*. When infants have their basic needs met, the attention with which to feel secure and you place those infants in a small group on a rug together they are gentle and kind with each other.

To further make a case for this type of wellness facilitation, so many people absorbed the benefit of such humane, kindness connectedness and heroism during this pandemic. Faced with the terrible pressures to survive this global health crisis, many people and companies around the world found beautiful ways to mean-ingfully be neighborly — to naturally act among the meek, and ever so helpfully mattering one to another without attention to color, gender, orientation, national origin, or any other differences.

I feel sorry for those in major leadership roles from around the world so perverted, s o t a k e n a w a y from this, their true essence. They are those who are facilitating disease spread, death, servitude and ugly supremacy from ignorant foundations and self-serving purposes. Had they not been deadened inside to their own true essence, they could have been leaders "of the heart." Instead, it is tragically sad the needless casualties, the magnitude, the extent of suffering and economic outfall happening from COVID-19.

New Zealand demonstrated leadership of the heart. Their COVID-19 consequences were dramatically less. People living their true nature as among the meek are free to vote for heart-based leadership. Those steeped in supremacist types of prejudice and hate are not. Regrettably, many of our United States citizens have been raised in harsh, authoritarian homes where allegiance to some form of supremacy reigns. Those poor souls usually experience dissonance and discomfort with heart based leadership. After all, their homes modeled the way things 'should' be. Their 'comfort zone' is immersion in a society that believes in punitive/vindictive, fear based, male dominated, enslaving and dictatorial leadership style. Check it out. Who have been the key 'controllers' in their lives? Religiously, culturally billions are raised to acquiesce to male authority figures. Most of those just take such style for granted and are discomforted otherwise.

※

9

Core Healing
DEPRESSION'S DARKNESS AND ANXIETIES' ATTACKS

THE NATIONAL INSTITUTE OF MENTAL HEALTH (NIMH) estimated in 2016 that 16.2 million U.S. adults had at least one major depressive episode. This represented 6.7 percent of the U.S. adult population, or about one household in any block of a dozen homes.

The number of episodes has considerably increased since then. Significantly, two populations are especially affected. There are the young people being overwhelmed with the challenge of being "good enough" or financially grounded enough to survive in today's world. The other is the financially floundering, white, middle-aged, less educated males. Their sense of inadequacy increases their angst, which amplifies their pain due to personal feelings of humiliation and anger with self. Depressive episodes result and escalate in intensity.

How do people escape the ever-intensifying angst, the resulting self-recrimination, the pain that heightens depression? That pain is amplified by the sometimes realistic fear that they aren't prepared to do what life in today's world requires of them to survive. They're simply not good enough, not up to the challenge. Thus, drinking, drugging, vaping, lack of self-care, overeating and suicide all go hand in hand to escape life's increasingly painfilled ideas about the demands of unattainable types of success required for life itself.

These increasingly challenging requirements to survive are robbing people of joy. How can one be happy when feeling too ill-equipped to do something about their own suffering let alone about how to help in a world that appears to be on fire both internally and externally? It leaves one feeling inadequate to the challenge and far too tired to even think straight.

Looking to find fault outside themselves — ways outside themselves to alleviate pain provoked by feelings of inadequacy — many males of all races are leaning into ever more savaging self-definitions of what it means to be a man. Such definitions even include being okay with raping or murdering women plus molesting children. All are pathetic forms of salve, a release from the hormonal surges demanding frequent release from tensions derived from the threat of feeling fundamentally dis-empowered and where their primal survival needs are challenged.

Then too, more and more white people, often males, who feel inadequate are turning to being some form of supremacist, and joining such groups as neo-Nazis. Then there are Incels who fault females when it's their own unwittingly enacted 'unlovability'. Many of these men deal with inadequacies' pain by wanting to take control of others through some form of dominance.

Even wealthy males can feel the pain of an inherent sense of being a loser because, in their mind, they are never able to be rich enough to be declared 'the' winner. Twenty or so years ago, I was working with a wealthy guy who when explaining his need for more and more money said: "You see Dr. Glasser, it's like a football game. The guy with the most money gets the touchdown. He's the hero of the game; he's the winner." Of regrettable interest to note, love not just being a 'winner' escaped him too due to living a transactional, companion for hire type marriage. Too bad we don't take seriously what the warning of worshiping the golden calf actually costs.

Of course, women too are by no means immune from depression. The sources of affliction are the same: anger with self, feeling out-of-control, as well as feeling hopeless, powerless, and useless. Such identities foster anxiety and depression for both males and females. Resulting drug abuse and suicide are growing. Immunity happens through wellness self-concepts that support a balanced life, beliefs that counteract, and skills that are 'anti-anxietying' and 'anti-depressing'. As Oprah would advise: "Live with an attitude of gratitude."

Assessing for Depression Resolution

Clinically and culturally *people have learned how to suffer.* Illness self-concepts foster misery. Negative beliefs developed lead people to seven of our cultural, learned sources of depression. Each and every one of these seven is addressed in one Core Healing session with each and every depressed client, male or female. Identifying which of these are at stake can lead to thorough resolution. In summary, such a core healing, hypno-analytic approach is first diagnostic then resolving. The learned sources of depression are:

1. Anger with self
2. Feeling out of control
3. Feeling powerless
4. Feeling useless
5. Feeling hopeless
6. Feeling helpless
7. Desire for secondary gain (being depressed to assert some self-serving purpose like financial survival or spousal manipulation).

Understanding Today's Context for Depression's Increase

In today's world, such feelings as those above are amplified the more we realize it's the amoral corporate, money / power driven, the bonus seeking CEOs plus their stockholders at customer expense who *matter* in our country and in our world, but not you and me. In other words, there are good CEOs like Bob Chapman, the Everybody Matters guy, or the "only I and mine who matter ones". The you corporate slave, me corporate profiteer type.

After the Second World War, we the people mattered but around 1980 through to 2010, we blatantly no longer did. In an erroneous Supreme Court decision, the business world finally accomplished superseding the people. "We the people" was absented in favor of "we the corporation."

Can our war on COVID-19 cause "we the people" to see enough kindly neighborliness to embolden us to demand that's the world we want b a c k for ourselves and our children? Such thoughtful, creative acts of kindness is what wellness in action has been looking like. We have been witnessing beautiful behavior from everyday folks. Rightly, those who have also put their lives on the line for people they don't even know have been major heroes. All these actions say *You Matter*. That type of kindly collective action commitment plus heart based leadership would lead to our being able to put ourselves back in healthier control of our lives in a way that makes them worth living.

It is our decision to make. Do we want that leadership of the heart (Franklin D. Roosevelt)? Or, are we going back to "business" as usual? Only with wise leadership such as FDR offered would this ever darkening cloud of depression lift and dissipate. But collectively, we have to assure all our votes count on behalf of wellness leadership at all levels of government.

Throughout human history, there have been the masters and the slaves. Money is amassed to buy empowerment. That's where, blindingly, we have been herded over the last four decades. All the components for democracy's rule are being undercut so that us ordinary folks will realize too late that we've been had. Then, we will be merely trudging through existence, even more tired, too tired to lift our heads, too tired to love, too tired to experience joy. How depressing is that? Look at the preceding list of seven. That's how slaves, regardless of age, regardless of settings, feel. Depression has even evolved genetically in some families. Depression has been perpetuated in families by the beliefs inherent in those seven depression inducing identities listed on page 113. The mind thusly gets imprinted with depression's locale(s) in the brain.

Far too many minds have been systematically propagandized so as to be willing yet unwitting slaves. That's how the "you don't matter" identity is being metastasized within.

People are being sold on the idea, they are subversively being made to believe they will succeed *but only if* they work hard. Work hard? So hard you are anxious? So hard you are too tired to sleep? So hard you are hardly home and hardly know your own children? That hard? So hard it makes you a communist or a socialist for objecting? Or are you neither? You're just someone who wants a better deal.

Working that hard makes people too tired with exhausting demands to even have the time to think straight. Depression's door is wide open welcoming us under such circumstances. One's mind is left available to the trash of tabloid news outlets that are about

money and power for the Publishers. They certainly are not about you or me. They have played fast and loose with the truth. When they are in newsprint form it's easier to spot the ridiculousness of the lies sensationalized. Now, tabloid news outlets are slicker and earning a fortune off those they addicted over the last decade or so.

Tabloid news outlets are much more sophisticated in suckering us to be ignorant to the real and additional sources of our pain, anxiety and depression. This fostered ignorance to actual truth is literally killing us. I am hoping this book helps to improve your life and that of our children by getting clarity about illness producing beliefs that thrive in fears' muddied conspiracies all the rage these days.

On the other hand, depression and anxiety lift and are more easily held at bay when you "mattering" is enacted. That means actualizing wellness beliefs more and more. By doing so, we can better protect ourselves from lies that many of our current leaders spew routinely. They have been stealing our dignity, our system of justice and the importance of good government of, by and for the people.

And, very critically, they have been stealing our wherewithal to survive and thrive as among the meek. Supremacy, its enemy, is being stoked instead.

Among the bad news of rioting due to over 400 years of ugly racism plus those riding on the coattails of the awfulness by physically destroying black owned shops, in that midst, here is the good news. As mentioned a bit ago, we are now witnessing something wonderful every day. People are spontaneously creating marvelous ways of saying to each other *You Matter*.

Here's but one of thousands of examples. A guy has been using his quarantine time at home fulfilling on-line requests from a website he created offering free greeting cards with flowers on them. He painted each by hand. Then, he addressed an envelope, put on a stamp and mailed them based upon requests received at his website. These cards were usable for any occasion a person wanted. After all, flowers no matter the occasion say: *You Matter*.

Thousands are spontaneously thinking of wonderful ways to reach out to each other. It has been uplifting. It is the opposite of depressing even during the treachery and tragedy of our Coronavirus pandemic along with supremacist drum beating. I am humbled by the outpouring of human decency. Standing tall in the face of natural fear, it has been heartening to see so many people enacting their fundamental nature as caring, kind, heroic, humane beings.

In spite of the cancerous outcomes when illness based beliefs are embraced, I am grateful to witness a growing, keener appreciation for mental health beliefs as evidenced by our country's everyday heroes. They are legion. Those with this spirit are the ones we must select as our governmental representatives.

Out of all this chaos, another heartening sight is seeing mental health moved to the front burner. Hopefully, as detailed in Part Three of this book, we will select government representatives at every level, who will afford each community, every neighborhood with equally and outstandingly equipped mind-body wellness centers so that anxiety, depression and suicide are dealt severe blows.

Empower Yourself: Know How Depression Comes About

What you believe leads you into — or out of — being depressed. It is an emotional state caused by negative self-concepts and beliefs that result in feelings such as:

- Helplessness
- Joylessness
- Powerlessness
- Grief
- Resentfulness
- Remorsefulness
- Worthlessness
- Uselessness
- Hopelessness
- Anger, mostly with self
- Despair

Regrettably, and all too often, feelings of unhappiness become these types of self-concepts. It's not hard to imagine the result of a child raised in a joyless home where, for one example, no one's birthday is celebrated. One inference could well be that life is meant to be lived joylessly. Depending on how many contributive beliefs are demonstrated, and how many of them the child comes to accept as truth, that child can grow up being very good at joyless living.

<u>If we don't want to have depression, we have to stop teaching children how</u>. How not to teach depression as a style of existence requires fundamental changes within ourselves. After all, we ourselves have been students. We have to unlearn these lessons.

I learned how to depress, how to do anxiety, how to do martyr, etc. Spending formative years following the how of it all gave me plenty of rehearsal time. Not pretty to admit but proud to be doing better though mightily challenged mid 2020 and into 2021.

To undo such awful lessons has taken me a lifetime of practicing better ways of being. I chose models to imitate. I chose the Reverend Martin Luther King, Jr. for nonviolence. A key source of depression is the violence that one does to oneself with self-inflicted ugly self-talk. I imitated his idea of forgiveness. I don't condone. But, I do my best not to linger in the pain and anger of a situation.

I chose movie heroes like Ali Baba as to how to lead with a sense of humor and enthusiastic follower-ship just not the thief part. Also, I decided not to be a martyr. That one, I did pretty easily. I thought it was such yucky behavior. Other self-chosen growth goals took me longer.

Just knowing that I don't have to be what I learned to believe as the way it is, is a lesson unto itself. I love when I hear myself or others referencing unhealthy behavior with the words "I used to." The longer my list of "I used to(s)," of my self-chosen ways to change, literally, the happier I am.

Most people don't know that they can set such behavioral wellness change goals and accomplish them. Strategies for each one and how to change it can be up to the individual. Becoming a nonsmoker took me years. My strategy was focused on decreasing the number of cigarettes I'd allow myself each day. In those days, I was one of the believers in nicotine as addictive so I cut back little by little until I could no longer give myself the excuse of being an addict.

When I chose to improve being a kind and thoughtful person, I again used a movie to teach me. I had watched another 'oldie but goodie'. There was the one with Jane Wyman and Rock Hudson called: Magnificent Obsession. In addition to becoming more kind it also inspired my being a doctor dedicated to easing pain and suffering in this world.

Easing pain and suffering is something you'd love to accomplish yesterday. In reality, I found a way to do my best utilizing my unique strengths and abilities just as I advise others to do with theirs. One of mine was being highly analytical. Like the doctor in the movie, I became a 'brain surgeon' but of the psychological sort. I'd remove tumorous beliefs and repair the locale with PRDs.

When what you focus on and develop as a strategy to change so as to not do depression or any behavior or emotion associated with it especially such as anger with self, when your strategies don't foster helpful change, then ideally there would be your neighborhood wellness center to teach you further skills in overcoming any of the basics of depression plaguing you.

While those seven basics of depression on page 113 are more or less causal for each person suffering from it, nonetheless, depression can look different on each of us because each of us can have somewhat varying constellations of self-concepts and beliefs. That variance, in part, accounts for the depth of such negative feelings experienced and types of depressive reactions undertaken. When you read Ken's case study, it will offer an example of what is explained here.

To recap, the most common undercurrent for depression is anger with self though lately not mattering due to powerlessness is likely superseding. It has to do with self-blaming for something internally believed and judged as shameful or as not good enough. As children, when judged as "bad" and consequently shamed and punished, the imprint for the ways that wrongs are handled is vengeful (punishing)in style. It is simply a cause/effect learned scenario as a set of beliefs.

When the individual is grown, the negative, "lessons" as   beliefs imprinted in childhood can be   self-righteously carried forward. They worsen and intensify because punishment doesn't work and as many of us have come to believe more is better. The self-punishment can become brutal. Of all the lessons I have learned while conducting hypno-analytics, perhaps the most horrific is a kind of brutality that is wrapped in self-imposed punishment that people enact upon themselves. Resultantly, it becomes anxiety producing, self-harming even to the extent of being physically damaging, cancer causing and/or just plain exhausting. *Consciously, unless otherwise educated, people are totally **unaware** of this damaging punishment they are doing to themselves.*

Most often the expression: "the punishment fits the crime" applies. Such depth of anger with self can result from not being able to find a job that will feed them and their children, or not having money needed to retire, not finding a mate, the loss of a lover, or about anything that causes any of us to experience such unhappy feelings as above.   Without intervention,   such   feelings   progress   from helplessness to uselessness, to hopelessness, and into despair. At its worst, despair leads to suicide.

People who are depressed often experience the condition of living with little or no pleasure in their everyday life. Often, they believe they don't deserve or should not be permitted to experience plea-sure. As time passes, and the number of supportive negative beliefs develop their constellations, people increasingly abandon the part of themselves that used to like to play and have fun —that is if they ever were allowed to be okay with experiencing joy in the first place.

Some self-concepts and beliefs that contribute to becoming depressed include:

- I've always been sad and lazy and see my life as meaningless.
- I feel spiritually disconnected.
- I give up too easily and feel like a failure.
- I'll never get better. I feel so powerless.

- I'm afraid of change and of being wrong. I'm angry with myself for being so dumb.
- My feelings are easily hurt.
- I have a hard time accepting help from other people. I don't trust them.
- I can't say no when people ask me to do things.
- I am a depressed person.
- I don't know how to be happy.
- Nothing I do is good enough.
- I can't relax and enjoy life.
- If I'm not doing everything perfectly, I don't feel I deserve to be happy.
- 'Depressing' (as in decompressing) is a great escape from the intensity of stress (mania), resulting from the supreme, failing effort to be perfect.
- I'm a workaholic.
- Food comforts me.

These beliefs summon depressive type reactions as listed on page 113. To have those as visible reactions requires bodily mechanics to cooperate with the fostering constellation of beliefs' enactment. The computer brain enacts the mind's collected beliefs that cascade that physiological chain of responses. If anger with self happens frequently, chemical imbalance might occur. Medication may help stabilize the imbalance but does not cure the belief or constellation of beliefs causing it in the first place. Brain rewiring must occur for healing.

Anxiety Feelings Amplify Depression

Children witness — often without the moderation of wellness oriented judgment — and absorb ideas along with visual imprints from whatever is going on around them, including how to gin up anxiety. Children learn ways of thinking about things and, subsequently, believing in them. Example: One evening, a little girl witnesses her dad trying to get their mom to try a new experience, such as a form of partner dancing, as opposed to the solo syncopated dancing they generally do together. The child observes the mother's manner of opposition to what is for her a scary idea. Her shrinking away can teach her daughter the fear of looking foolish. The resulting belief: I fear looking foolish or being ridiculed when trying something new.

In the future, when approached to try something new in front of others, the youngster will likely decline. If she is pushed upon with an "aw, come on" suggestion, anxiety can erupt. If she is pushed really hard, depression from feeling out-of-control can surface.

Parents aren't always aware of what in fact their children are absorbing from their behavior. How parents do or do not express themselves, how they walk, talk, dress, and interact teaches beliefs. Some of that behavior expressly teaches how to feel anxiety or reap anxiety followed by depression. Thus, over time, emotional disorders can take on a genetic appearance and/or change.

Another way to augment a child's ability to "do" anxiety and depression is by the mismanagement of a child's normal sense of caution, their fear of the unknown and their internal realization they would die if left alone. Some key junctures that require wise handling by adults include: starting school, a parent leaving on a business trip, mom or dad losing a job and relocating, or losing a beloved grandparent. If parents mismanage preparing their children, the children will imitate how to mismanage them too. Absorbing the generative beliefs also occurs.

It can't be said often enough: Children learn foundational response patterns by example. They learn "how to" anxiety and "when to" get depressed. They absorb the thought patterns and foundational beliefs that produce the anxiety and depression.

The same is true for sex patterning. This is how males "do" anxiety and depression. This is what females do. Depression, as an attention getter, is also learned: "Oh, poor thing, she's always so unhappy."

Depression seemingly takes on some of the attributes of what is referred to as a bad habit. But, it is the escalating number of the reinforcing beliefs that still govern in the same stimulus, same response fashion. Over and over again and from each relevant time to another such time, the same belief dictated behavior and emotion evidences itself.

Children learn depression from their parents in many ways. Most people are excited about becoming parents and want to do the best job possible. But what we've seen is that if they want to be perfect parents, their children must act perfectly. Imagine this: A child brings home a report card with four A's and one B. The B gets all the attention. The child gets the additional implicit, awful identity developing message, "No matter how well I do, it's never good enough." That's one scenario that guides a child to the erroneous conclusion: "Well, I must be perfect to be loved or appreciated." It holds the power of placing a self-flagellating whip in the child's hand.

Children of "perfect parents" often hear things like, "Is that what you're planning to wear today? I thought I taught you to dress better than that." Again, the pressures provoke anxiety and depression. The stress of needing to be perfect grows and can become chronic. Depression follows as the child feels more out-of-control. These children become powerless to please and more and more angry with themselves for not knowing how to be perfect. I call perfectionism a disease. I would concur with any colleague who would say Bi-Polar Disorder is one result.

Another way parents inadvertently foster anxiety and depression is by doing everything for their children. They don't allow children to do chores. They say things like: "No, no, I'll take care of that. I'll do it." Then children don't learn basic life skills, which interferes with one's competence in living independently.

Parents can be overly helpful with homework, sometimes doing it for the child. Allowances are given without having the child earn it or guiding them in how to manage money wisely.

Parents may clean the child's room and protect him or her from any sort of work that is 'beneath them." A sense of ugly entitlement ensues. Either the parents or "the help" do all the cleaning, cooking, laundry, and bill paying. Later, when those children need those essential life skills, they're lost. They don't have the basic fundamentals for survival on their own. And socially, they often treat others in the helping professions as an underclass of servants or underlings. Calling them "snobs" won't fix that problem.

Bottom line: These children grow up being the unfortunate and, in their own way, the anxious and unhappy ones. They don't know how to cope with life and natural and/or cultivated fears when venturing out into the world. The expression, there's a "failure ready to launch" at times applies. Such identities can leave them with frantic feelings such as:

"I don't know how to do this."

"I don't know how to get by without help."

Again, the result can be significant anxiety, which can lead to depression and dependency. The greater the intensity and duration of the anxiety, together with the more out of control and angry people feel with themselves, the more depressed they become.

Common Anxiety Producing Negative Self-Concepts and Beliefs

In the discovery phase of core healing, while note taking, I circle each of the actual negative self-concepts and beliefs that explain a client's "why's." Those that produce both anxiety *and* depression include:

- "I do most things wrong. I feel so helpless. I must be a hopeless case."
- "There is something wrong with me."
- "I'm not good enough. (linked, of course, to: "I have to be perfect.")
- "I don't matter." (Or, "I don't matter anymore.")
- "I'm worthless."
- "I deserve to be abandoned."
- "I am angry with myself and deserve to be severely punished for my mistakes. Consequently, I abandoned my creative passion."
- "I'll be sent to Hell."
- "I can't relax and enjoy life. Idle hands are the devil's workshop".
- "I'm unlovable."
- "I am winding up alone, without any close friends."
- "I can't take the pain of such disappointment of being left again."
- "I'll get fat to protect myself." (It's what I call: "fat as fortress.")
- "I don't have a right to be happy."

CASE STUDY: KEN

Ken suffered from severe depression. He had done cognitive therapy with minimal results and didn't want to start antidepressants. He didn't know where to turn, and a friend recommended Core Healing with me.

Ken was always tired. His friends told him, "You have to get out of the house!" But he always made excuses. During what he called the "dark times," he couldn't leave the bed or the couch. He didn't exercise, barely had enough energy to get to work, and when he got home collapsed in front of the television to watch TV with an array of junk food snacks. Ken cried a great deal. He drank more than he knew was healthy and was sixty pounds overweight. Though smart,

Ken had difficulty in school. Despite this, he continued as he was expected to. That persistence worked out well. To keep himself from getting bored, he became a computer technician, which he was pretty good at doing. After gradu-ation, Ken got a job as a "techy."

No matter how well Ken's boss said he was doing, Ken's interpretation of his own performance was that it was less than perfect and, therefore, not good enough. He didn't get it right fast enough. Sometimes, his work was improved upon by someone in a quality control position. Overall, though, his annual evaluations kept him employed.

Ken almost got married about a year after he first started working. The girl he had become serious about left him for one of the guys from work that she met at a party Ken took her to.

Over time, these "not good enough" feelings magnified due to subsequent experiences causing Ken to further judge himself as being less than perfect. Such judgment was always depressingly lurking in the background, eventually playing havoc with the physical, emotional, behavioral, and relational aspects of his life.

In one of the core healing sessions, during the discovery phase, Ken was asked this question: What is the most criti-cal, most relevant memory to "Why have I come to feel so nervous at work?" The memory that came up while in the heightened self-awareness state was this:

Client: I am on the football field.

Therapist: How old are you in this memory?

Client: About 14.

Therapist: What in this memory is occurring to you?

Client: My coach is walking over to me.

Therapist: What happened next?

Client: My football coach, who moved his head in a sad side-to-side gesture said: "*Son, you'll just never amount to anything* playing football, even though you clearly have worked really hard! I recommend you try soccer."

Ken was traumatized by that statement, and those italicized words imprinted right into his brain-body as a self-concept. Alternatively, the coach would have been much more compassionate, much wiser had he said something like: "Ken, I think your talents will be better used at soccer than football. Can I be your coach for that instead? Soccer practice is on Tuesdays and Thursdays after school."

Unfortunately, it was that imprinted statement: "You'll never amount to anything" that became a terrible identity actualized by Ken in various ways over time. That is one way his perfectionism-related constellation of negative self-concepts and beliefs grew. No matter how hard, how perfectly he tried to do well, he'd never amount to anything. How depressing is that?

Compounding the problem was losing his girlfriend, especially to someone at work. Now, he was unlovable too. Increasing amounts of anxiety and depression developed as these "weed seeds" sprawled. He began treating himself more and more poorly, as if he just didn't matter anymore.

After all, how does it feel to blame yourself, more frequently over time, for never amounting to much of anything because you thought of yourself as imperfect, no matter how hard you tried? Powerless in his inability to matter!

Over time, that host of supportive negative beliefs grew. They became actualized in an ever widening, cancerous way throughout Ken's life. They grew into a constellation of negative, anxiety provoking, out of control, angering at self, depressing self-concepts and beliefs that included:

- "I'm worthless."
- "My opinion doesn't count."
- "I won't ever have somebody to love me."
- "I'm a loser."
- "I'll never do anything of consequence with my life."
- "I might as well be dead."
- "No woman will ever want a man like me."

One by one, in the healing phase, these negative self-concepts and beliefs were replaced with their positive opposites. The hypnotic state allows ideas to be *uncritically* accepted as true when they are presented with compassionate context. Additionally, we "cognitively reframed" the incident with his coach, reliving the incident for the better. A wholesome style of forgiving and self-assertive ways of behaving, of man-to-man interacting became new imprints, the new Ken.

Additional positives were imprinted based upon Ken's strengths and lovability. Forgiveness was facilitated between him and his former love. Compassion for self was enhanced. Ways he could purpose his life, based upon having identified his variety of strengths, were highlighted. His "I don't matter unless perfect" identity was replaced with "I matter regardless because I have much to offer."

I talked with Ken recently, three years after our work together. This is what he said: "The depression is gone"! Realistically, he continued, "I do sometimes get anxious or depressed over something that is genuinely sad and scary like the worsening of the Coronavirus here in our country. At least now I know how to deal with it. It doesn't take me over."

And he continued: "I am also happy to report, I take much better care of myself." Continuing on Ken gushed: "I still work hard, but I have incredible energy. I laugh more. I even used to cry. Now, I work out with my friends, and one of them told me the other day, "Dude, you have so much more energy!" I don't dwell anymore on the negative. I wake up every day and take a run. I never did that! When I get home from work, I meditate instead of zoning out in front of the TV.

"My relationships are completely different. I used to avoid conflict with people. I'd say, 'Everything's good,' even when it wasn't. Now I voice my opinion. I'm straightforward. And, I don't hide or shy away from people anymore. I even have a few friends. My family sees a big change."

On a later follow-up call, after further needed Core Healing work, Ken said: "My food choices are different. I don't eat sugar, and I don't drink at all. I eat much less junk food. The greatest gift of core healing is that I'm so much more relaxed and empowered. I care about myself, which I never did. If things get tough, I just tell myself: Take a deep breath, stay in the moment, you'll work it out."

Then Ken added: "And, last evening, in the parking lot where I work, I left my keys in the car. Before, I would have gone ballistic. It would have been the end of the world. But

I just said to myself, 'Let's not make it into a big deal. Don't get down on yourself.' Before, I would have said, "What a jackass!" Instead, I just called AAA and then called my brother to catch up with him while I waited. I transformed the negative situation into something positive.

"It's all just so amazing."

Hearing outcomes like this, I wish everyone could benefit from core healing. It is a powerful and relatively swift process for marvelous wellness outcomes. In addition, there are other ways we are able to improve.

To reduce anxiety and depression in our lives, the bottom line is that *we have to shift allegiance to wellness based beliefs.* We must weed out teaching and exemplifying beliefs that we have taken for granted as "good," and as pain relievers. Those "pain relievers," whether benign or ugly like vengeance , will work if you believe they do. But there are far better ways to insulate against pain, to reduce the hurt, and to protect ourselves from illness. We simply do not have to embrace, teach, or exemplify the anxiety and depression producing beliefs.

So, yes, the quality of *your* life does matter. You can either be a Loving Energy source lighting freedom's path. Or, your life *can be* emblematic of the pain defined by the "dark," the illness side. Living a *you matter 'purposed for wellness'* life will humanely grow you and our culture into a true liberty beacon.

It's time for racism and the idea that only whites matter to reside once and for all in the dustbin of our history. Such illness beliefs have caused enormous amounts of pain and suffering not just to the receivers but to the loveless, arrogant, empty, ignorant, cruel doers. As a white woman, I cannot claim 100% innocence. But I can claim total abdication of the ugly of it as well as a total embrace for permanent changes for the better.

When I look into the eyes of those either indifferent to or the perpetrators of such suffering of others, I see dead souls. With what kind of ignorance were they raised? The answer quite simply: ignorance of wholesome living. The information is here with which to bring meaningful life to our newborns. Let's not let our children suffer in the arrogance of indifference to suffering. Our world is dying. Let us bring it back to life better than ever.

❄

10

Escaping Pain and Despair
SUBSTANCE ABUSE AND SUICIDE

SUBSTANCE ABUSE IS about self-medicating one's psychic and/or physical pain and enduring suffering. It may be used to at least temporarily subdue one's fears and sad feelings. Ironically, it can also be a way people attempt to control something that can never be in their control. The NRD = I need to be other controlled.

Substance abuse is learned by observation, as a way to soothe emotional and physical pain, and as an inappropriate way to deal with fear. Alcohol and cannabis dis-inhibit and allow one to let loose with anger or acting sexy, or socializing or whatever. These substances overcome identities like being *shy* (not feeling safe with others), *raging,* being *silly, making jokes,* etc.

Dis-inhibiting drugs can also allow one to experiment with something they fear like doing other, more escapist, more dangerous street or prescribed drugs like 'oxi'. How dangerous the behavior depends upon how much that person feels they might matter or don't matter at all.

For this latter dis-inhibiting reason alcohol and cannabis are called "gateway drugs." They remove the fear one was taught about the pitfalls of getting physiologically addicted to a dangerous to life drug. If one's identity is that he or she doesn't matter at all, a killer street drug is used to OD their way out of life, i.e., suicide.

With a gateway drug, the experimenting v e r s u s s u i c i d a l person is then *carefree* to do what they actually want to do but have been shoving down, which means *there can be both pro and con beliefs warring internally.* Some refer to that warring as between their better angel on one shoulder and the devil on the other.

Substances like food, alcohol or drugs may be used to numb pain, even if only temporarily. They can give people a minimal sense of control or escape in the short term. But sooner rather than later, abusing substances makes the abuser feel even more out of control, more powerless. Substance abuse, in part, is an attempt to cope that almost always backfires and makes matters worse. The weed sprawl grows and, along with it anxiety and depression.

This phenomenon of making things worse can apply both to prescription, street drugs and other non-prescribed substances. Other misused, poor self-management tools include cigarettes, chewing tobacco, etc.

Getting Rid of Labels

We've seen how labels such as "depressed" or "anxious" can reinforce people's negative self-concepts and actually perpetuate these conditions. Where substance abuse is concerned, it is even more important to avoid labels. *Talking about one's "problems" with a substance implies the potential for an easier resolution.*

The words "addict" and "alcoholic" are thrown around very freely today. Using these words is not helpful. It invites people to think of themselves as "addicts" or "alcoholics," which makes things worse when they adopt negative attributes, NRDs associated with those labels. This means constellation additive beliefs such as being weak, helpless and powerless. As weak, helpless and powerless they will continue *abusing* their substance of choice *struggling* daily not to *succumb* (the conduct of an addict), fearing relapse and increasing feelings of depression.

In this example, the identity of the *alcoholic* expands. Their negative belief constellation grows. Now, they are not just drinkers but they abuse alcohol, struggle to quit and surrender to temptation. And, if they dare take a drink, they relapse completely. They are back to square one.

Alcoholics Anonymous, Overeaters Anonymous, Narcotics Anonymous, plus other twelve step programs have good intentions when they invite people to introduce themselves as "an alcoholic" or "an addict." They want to get people out of denial about their unhealthy dependencies. The problem with this practice is that the self-concepts of "I'm an addict" or "I'm an alcoholic" get reinforced each time they introduce themselves. It continues to define them and *creates more of a problem*. Being "addicted" implies that, at best, it will be difficult to stop. And, more likely, life will become a daily, painful struggle siren calling the substance of choice's abuse.

I don't want Core Healing to be difficult. I ask people who come for substance abuse management to stop referring to themselves as "addicts." Instead, I urge them to think of themselves as people with a problem. I can't repeat that idea often enough. We all have problems, and problems can be solved — sometimes, even quite easily. We've all heard people say, "I used to drink (or smoke, or use drugs), but I don't do that anymore." So, rather than introducing themselves as "an alcoholic," it might be better to say something like, "My name is Amy and I have a problem with alcohol." That sounds far more hopeful and encouraging to resolve.

By the way, people with a severe drinking problem, created it when they made the decision to drink specifically for the purpose of "getting drunk" to the point of being "out of it" on a regular basis. This is a different decision than that of a person who drinks to take the edge off when socializing or when relaxing. Their self-concept is that of a social drinker.

As indicated, a "drunk" is more likely dealing with significant emotional pain, anxiety, depression and intense fears such as powerlessness. Alcohol depresses because hung over such feelings are reinforced.

But a "drunk" can also be a 'like father like son' identity or, 'like mother like daughter.' It becomes identity imitation.

A "social drinker" may be dealing with one degree or another of anxiety. More precisely, that type of social drinker is dealing with the fear of feeling safe around people especially with those they do not particularly know.

The Roots of Substance Abuse

As seen, substance abuse has many roots. Some of the most common listed and to be discussed in more detail are:

SHYNESS ON STEROIDS

Shyness is a huge contributor to substance abuse — especially the substances of alcohol and marijuana, the dis-inhibitors. The self-concept, "I am shy," is usually imprinted in childhood.

As animal beings, we are naturally wary of strangers and those who are bigger than us. When children are introduced to their parents' friends, little children often "shy away" and try to hide. A son can be told, "now son don't be shy!" Then the parent turns to his friend and compounds the problem with, "Oh, you have to excuse Bobby, he's shy." That is a huge mistake. Being "shy" — think about what behavior that identity calls for. It requires isolation to be safe.

From our example, w h a t Bobby needs in that moment is to be *complimented* on being smart due to his appropriate *caution*. It's the "stranger danger" message children are taught on how to guard themselves. That identity of being wisely cautious needs strengthening as cautious and wise, not weakening with the label "being shy."

We are hardwired to be cautious as part of our survival skills package. Though sadly, Bobby, like thousands of other children, now has that potentially crippling self-concept that he is a shy person.

Shyness is terribly uncomfortable and can result in isolation. Bobby will do whatever he can to manage the resulting discomfort of loneliness as well as the conflicting fear of being alone. If he fails to overcome his shyness, he may become more reclusive and introverted. When he is older, he may use alcohol and marijuana. These drugs reduce the inhibition to socialize. Vapers have often begun smoking to "be one of the gang." Cigarette smokers use the cigarette as their companion.

Fundamentally, human beings are not loners. Loners are made, not born. It's our animal nature to band together whether we talk about flocks, droves, packs, schools or bands of brothers and sisters. We want to socialize and be part of a group. There's where a sense of security derives.

Bobby may use drugs or alcohol to overcome his shyness. What substances he chooses depends on his parents' substance abuse choices, or those of his high school friends and their parents. The degree of his fear, his other negative self-concepts and beliefs, as well as subsequent reinforcing events, will either amplify or de-emphasize dependency.

Clients who come to Core Healing for substance abuse often say things like, "I do well with socializing and having fun when I'm under the influence." "But when I'm not, I revert back to that other person, the shy person." How this statement can be interpreted is that they, in fact, have the social skills they need to have fun when relating to others just not the supportive identity.

They couldn't exhibit such skills if they didn't have them even under the influence. They just need to get rid of the negative self-concept of being "shy," so they can live in that truth. That way, a person's inherent need to socialize can allow the conscious mind's desire and decision to socialize comfortably and be more outgoing unimpeded by the negative self-concept of "shy." Any additional NRDs in the shyness constellation, when also deleted, result in no need for the drug of choice, at least not for the purpose of over-coming "shyness."

REBELLIOUS REACTIONS

Rebellious reactive decisions are also a frequent factor in substance abuse. Most parents tell their children they can't use substances like alcohol, nicotine and drugs. Or, they can't have dessert if they misbehave. One of the most common reactions is, "Oh yeah? Watch me!" Or "I'm old enough to do what I want!" Or "You can't make me!" Almost as night follows day, kids at times reach for what their parents forbid just to prove that they can.

This is partly an attempt to get control, something children and teens want desperately. "I'm in control of my own life. I can do what I want!" Of course interestingly, abusing substances almost always involves a loss of control. So, what's the actual identity?

LEARNED DEPENDENCE

We have noted frequently that when parents do everything for their children, the children never learn to take care of themselves. This learned dependence is an enormous factor in substance abuse.

Kids grow up with the self-concept, "I can't make it on my own." When they realize that the time is soon coming when they have to be out on their own, they become terrified. Quite often, they use substances to numb the fear of having to be responsible for their own life. Naturally, this makes the controlling parents feel as if they have lost control. In one extreme case, Karen started drinking and smoking pot at sixteen as a reaction to her overly controlling parents. She was just experimenting. But when her father caught her smoking pot, he took Karen to a mental institution to be treated for *addict*ion. This was serious overkill. Now Karen had the self-concept that she was an "addict" compounded by the identity "crazy."

Karen's case is dramatic. She and others intensely fear they can't make it on their own. Substance abuse follows as anxiety management. Around fifteen, they start getting anxious. Around eighteen, many will be expected to take care of themselves and/or live independently. They will either get a job or go off to college. This prospect can fill some youngsters with dread but others with terror. They are acutely aware that they don't know how to handle their money, their relationships, their schedule, their work, cooking, taking care of their space, or even doing their laundry seems beyond the capabilities or the identities of many.

Getting a job may feel overwhelming. Their mind computes, "I don't have a clue how to get along in life. I don't know how to earn a real living. I don't have an education. I don't even like school. What am I going to do?" Based on those type beliefs, what emotions logically result? The more lost the youngster feels, the more intense their fear based feelings become.

The closer those young people get to the time when they are expected to be out on their own, the higher their anxiety. They may turn to alcohol first. If that doesn't alleviate the anxiety, and if pot doesn't do it, they graduate to something stronger. Long before they are actually on their own, they have been through a progression of substances as their fears escalate and they dissolve into an "I don't matter anyway" frame of mind.

It is a predictable cycle. The learned helplessness creates anxiety and depression. Substances are an attempt to medicate the pain of helplessness, powerlessness and as a result depression and anxiety. The higher the anxiety and the deeper the depression, either binging or stronger drugs are used. Binging is symptomatic of stark terror. It is about being terrified of being absolutely unlovable... until one is guided to realize otherwise.

Until then, what doesn't change is that dependent types increase their dependence on something outside themselves. And it began with their parents and continued with the substances. Becoming dependent on a substance is a logical extension of being raised to see oneself as a dependent person — dependent on someone or something for survival.

Eventually, most do leave home but often they continue to medicate their anxiety and depression with substances well into adulthood. So long as the feeling remains that they aren't up to making it on their own or even having a loving partner to help, they continue to use external factors including people, circumstances, or substances that they empower to ' control' these emotions. Obviously, these alternatives do not fix anything. They just prove to the individual their frightening dependency.

This need to look outside themselves for control is learned dependency. Self-reliance has not been taught. Hovercraft parenting cripples. Becoming independent is a skill in itself.

When misguided parents dictate when and how everything should be done, down to the smallest detail rather than helping the child age appropriately to learn by doing, then a sense of learned helplessness ensues. When they are always looking outside themselves for authority and control, it may be only a matter of time before they reach for substances to at least feel a modicum of being in control. Therein lies a paradox.

When people get some small measure of temporary control and relief, they can start believing that their substance of choice is the reason they are able to manage or cope. They may even believe that if some of it is good, more must be better. They begin a process of collecting constellations of reinforcing beliefs about the value of the substance. Ultimately, of course, they feel betrayed and the substance itself becomes a problem. Their modicum of control evaporates. Their fears escalate.

NUMBING

People who are in emotional and physical pain are in a "_dis_-eased" state, meaning _not at_ ease. The pain may range from mild to intense. Its duration may be intermittent or constant. It would be great if an occasional aspirin was all that folks needed. Sadly, that is not the case.

Physicians have been putting forth a mighty effort to deal with pain management. So have psychotherapists, physical therapists, nurses, and all those dedicated to easing pain and suffering in the world. Be that as it may, the problem of pain both emotional and physical is raging out of control. Pill pushers make things worse. So millions of pills ingested, millions of gallons of alcohol consumed, millions of cigarettes smoked, millions of hours spent in one form of therapy or another aren't stemming the tide. Children and adults hurting physically and mentally are turning to street drugs, in frantic search of alleviation. Numbing, the escape from pain, is their goal.

Major sources of internal pain and discomfort are building. Steam builds similar to that of a pressure cooker within. Think of the image of a terrorist agreeing to wear an explosive vest and blowing himself to bits along with the designated 'enemies'. That is numbing one's sense of worthlessness in the extreme.

Potential beliefs that allowed this terrorist to overcome the powerful human drive for survival include this constellation of beliefs: There's a heaven; the cause is just; Allah will be welcoming; becoming a martyr is admired; it's the only way to be respected and to matter as a man; and, there are virgins ready to service me upon my arrival in heaven. That is delusional.

Obviously, numbing gives way to something more extreme at the point when the substance used no longer numbs enough. The goal of healing is curing the pain through eliminating its various sources. Collectively, these have here been referred to as constellations of beliefs. They emerge relatedly from the initial

NRD belief such as being not good enough that has acted like a magnet for additional and supportive beliefs.

Constellations accumulate related negative beliefs as one ages. The larger the constellation and the numbers of them, collectively they compound one's pain and suffering. And, without any sense of right or wrong (amorally) the mind-body executes these beliefs in response to related stimuli every waking moment and even into one's dreams at night. (As a result of Core Healing peoples' dreams improve meaning they become benign or even pleasant instead of discomforting, even nightmarish.)

Summary

Increasing substance abuse suggests more and more intense primal fears coming into play, such as being scared to death by acting in risky fashion. It involves not mattering due to associated feelings of abandonment, being unlovable, being alone, worthless as one shirks responsibility for oneself, feeling helpless, being shy, and even unworthy of existence. These beliefs, as fears, drive people toward addiction. Collectively, they are scary as any imagined hell.

Even though people with such dependency may believe that they deserve to be abandoned, they nevertheless want other people in their lives because loneliness can certainly be painful. They're seeking a peer group, and often they believe that the only group who won't reject them are other "addicts." These like minded souls are sometimes the only people who represent comfort and acceptance. For many, this is one factor that allows for the adherence to moving step by step forward in such groups as Alcoholics Anonymous, Overeaters Anonymous, or Narcotics Anonymous.

At some point, such folks hit bottom. They either die or change direction, guided by the help of some such type of recovery group. Often, these groups also teach practical and emotion management skills that people need in order to cope with life.

It is said that when someone starts abusing drugs or alcohol, their maturity is put on hold. With the support of groups that understand this dynamic, people can acquire better beliefs over time. They can learn how to be responsible for themselves, learn social skills, vocational skills, follow a twelve step type program toward building self-esteem, and better manage their emotions plus getting help with the other practical aspects of their lives such as a place to live and reconciliation with family.

In addition to the fears mentioned above, pain causing negative self-concepts and beliefs of people who abuse substances are:

- "I'm scared."
- "I am a rebel."
- "I am shy."
- "I have to be perfect."
- "I need to look 'macho' (by drinking a case of beer)."
- "I'm not good enough."
- "I need excitement because I feel so dead inside." (Danger provides excitement. Street drugs, for example, are a good way to find danger.)
- "I'm angry, and I don't know why."
- "I am empty and purposeless."
- "I have no defenses against a dangerous world."
- "I can't stop spinning my wheels."
- "I can't take care of myself and be on my own."
- "I'm afraid of success because I'll probably lose it."
- "Nobody will ever love me. I'll die alone."
- "I won't fulfill my purpose in life."
- "I need a substance (alcohol, drugs, food) to comfort me."
- "I deserve to be abandoned."
- "I'm unlovable."
- "I'm stupid."
- "I'm a nervous person."
- "I'm inadequate, weak and a loser."

- "I point out other people's flaws so mine won't be so obvious."
- "I am unmotivated and sad, so any progress I make is slow."
- "I don't know how to be responsible for, or in control of, myself."

The beauty of Core Healing is that it can go directly to the heart of the problem. I ask people who come to deal with substance abuse, "If you didn't have a headache, would you go to the medicine cabinet and take a couple of aspirin?" Of course they wouldn't. Then I ask, "So if you didn't have the anxiety or depression, and if you had a great job and were earning a good living, and felt able to handle life independently, and had loving friends, would you need that substance anymore?" Not likely. They wouldn't be in physical or emotional pain and could go forward into their lives with a sense of self-reliance and the self-satisfaction that comes from feelings of competence.

CASE STUDY: STAN

Stan was an inveterate smoker. He had tried to quit multiple times and failed until he finally heard of Core Healing. In addition to being "a die-hard smoker," he told me that cigarettes were a way to keep his anger in check and his weight down. They were also a way to take "mini breaks", and he admitted sheepishly to keeping others at a distance as well. "Smoking cigarettes fills up something in me that nothing else does," he said. I've heard many smokers label themselves "die-hards" (loners who generally die alone).

This self-definition compounds the problem. With that idea in place, they have to act out that definition. Quitting has to be extra-ordinarily hard, so hard they will die painfully. In other words, they may believe that is the way they are meant to die . . . the hard way. But Stan had a positive belief that enabled him to entertain the possibility that he could quit easily if we identified and deleted the negative self-concepts and beliefs that had led to his smoking and replace them with better ones . That is the job of the Core

Healer to facilitate.

Under hypnosis, Stan returned to the most critical, most relevant memory related to why he was committed to smoking. The memory that emerged was in his mother's womb. He felt himself suspended in the amniotic fluid and became aware that his mother was agitated and he felt nauseous. She was smoking. It's amazing that a fetus has such felt senses.

Then his mother told her husband, his father, that she was pregnant. The father became enraged and said, "How dare you get pregnant!" In the next instant, he savagely kicked his wife's belly. Even though Stan was suspended in and protected by the amniotic fluid, even though he had no language to even translate the experience as a fetus, he *felt* the turbulence and was terrified. He *felt* as if he shouldn't exist. Of course being kicked to death by someone you are dependent upon would certainly be a hard way to die. This self-concept was imprinted into his subconscious as a felt sense in the midst of that trauma.

We also uncovered a constellation of reinforcing beliefs, including:

- "I am terrified of those on whom I am dependent."
- "I'm a nervous person."
- "I don't trust others not to hurt me."
- "I'm unworthy of being loved, not good enough."
- "At times, I feel like an outcast."
- "I am weak/defenseless."
- "I deserve to be abandoned."

Smokers often have these or similar negative self-concepts and beliefs. In addition, as they grow up, they observe other smokers. Their subconscious absorbs the belief that their kind of uneasiness and discomfort can be managed with cigarettes – just as it seems to be the case for those they observe. Even though quite the opposite is true. After all, it *appears* to be the case.

Nicotine is actually a stimulant, not a relaxant. And, nicotine constricts the blood vessels, which means the heart has to pump harder. But the mind-body is in charge of the bio ecosystem. So, these biochemically operationalized beliefs make smoking *seem and actually feel* like it's relaxing because that mind-body control over-rides the true physical reaction and the individual is more relaxed.

Additionally, smoking becomes relaxing because smokers are briefly *distracted* from the stress of the moment *during the ritualistic time it takes to reach for, find, withdraw, and light up the cigarette.* Once it is lit, *then* the mind can focus on one's thoughts. Since the mind can only focus on one thing at a time, the act of getting and lighting up the cigarette distracts from the fray of one's thoughts. It's the body that can "walk and chew gum at the same time."

After deleting Stan's smoker negatives, and replacing in his subconscious with the constellation of beliefs that he needed to become a nonsmoker, he was free to actualize his new identity. So, I ask you: Do nonsmokers have any difficulty rejecting the offer of a cigarette? No. Why? Stan was now able to easily reply: "Because I am not a smoker anymore."

Stan said at the end of our sessions, "I can't believe I gave all that power to a piece of paper with dried leaves rolled up in it."

Even after he stopped smoking, Stan found that his hands were restless. They kept fidgeting, and he had trouble holding them still. I asked him what he had liked doing with his hands over the course of his life, other than smoking. He said, "You know, when I was a little boy, I used to like to whittle." At the time he said this, he was in his sixties. "As a matter of fact, I know a whittling class that's just starting. I could learn more there. Whittling would sure be more fun to do with my hands when sitting on the back porch than smoking."

Once people are free from the negative self-concepts and beliefs that drove them to the substance, they have a lot more energy to be creative and lead more fulfilling lives.

Suicide Sources

Suicide's sources include unrelenting pain, despair, a total sense of aloneness, feeling unlovable, vengeance (the punishment of self or others), a total sense of not mattering, being useless, a desperate attempt to matter, martyrdom, the escape to a "better place," or consigned to hell where they believe they belong and feeling totally out of control as in being "freaked out scared."

Suicide's potential tools: deadly substances; cops (suicide by cop); Covid; risky driving behavior (menacing, racing driving style); bridges high enough to jump off of; becoming a soldier; picking a fight with the 'wrong' person; starving oneself to death; etc.

An important aside: The number one formally named mental illness killer is Anorexia. An anorexic's death is not likely a suicidal outcome as some think. Death is more likely the result of a negative reactive decision like this one from a client I worked with at a psychiatric hospital. "I have to have the body of a boy". Why? "So my father will rough house with me as we used to and the way he still does with my brother." (Her body was maturing. The father had appropriately responded by backing away from playing that way.)

Innocently, this immaturely derived belief causing starvation to achieve was a terrible life threatening consequence scaring all concerned. With Core Healing, her identity was returned to being comfortable as a lovable young woman free to otherwise experience her father's love. She was free to eat healthfully again. She was weaned off the feeding tube up her nose as her engagement with eating again returned. Slowly, she was guided to eat on her own. Two and one half weeks later, she was released from the hospital.

11

Living Life Lovingly and Well
A CONTRACT WITH SELF

THERE ARE marital and business contracts. At the age of four, I had no idea of the notion of a contract. Regardless, I made one with myself. As a result, the rest of my life, I found I liked being a caring person. It was what I call a fortunate positive reactive decision. How did it happen?

My father asked me this question: What is antidisestablishmentarianism? Really? Yes, he did. If you knew my dad and how he raised me, you wouldn't be surprised.

When my dad asked me that question, I had absolutely no idea what he was talking about. Being only four years of age, my beliefs developed up until then popped these words out of my mouth: "It means being a caring person." My father looked down at me with an approving smile. I felt proud of myself for getting his affectionate, approving and warm smile.

So, too young to actually judge the wisdom of my commitment, I was lucky. To please my dad, I birthed an acorn seed, a PRD (a positive reactive decision), a contract for life. I became a forever caring person.

As Fred Rogers said: "Love isn't a state of perfect caring. It is an active noun, similar to struggle. To love someone is to strive to accept that person exactly the way he or she is — here and now." Caring seems to be about unconditional acceptance. In any event, I have found being a caring person a worthy goal to grow in my life.

A person I recently met made expressing that identity easy. I felt honored to be able to evidence being a caring person with a colleague I admire, Dr. Kimberly Besuden. From age four until now in my senior years that acorn seed has grown so that it's not about me, it's about what I admire and support in others. I care about the goodness, the wealth of person hood with which they are able to give us of their wisdom.

I have Dr. Besuden's permission to share what she wrote and am proud to do so because she evidenced a similar contract with herself. She is a truly caring person. While there are many in healing professions, there are few that raise it to the level of art, as does Dr. Besuden.

Kimberly Besuden
Doctor of Chiropractic
Certified Functional Medicine Practitioner
American Clinical Board of Nutrition (pending)
Clinical Hypnotherapist Certification (pending)

The pandemic effect of COVID-19 has altered life for everyone. While we have been in a crisis at this moment, I see an extraordinary future for wellness opportunities. The pandemic has created a new normal, changing how we manage business, education, and family from this point on. We have new possibilities to thrive by creating amazing circumstances for humankind.

Over the first months the disease spread, I watched my

family, friends, and patients go through three phases. First, there is overwhelming fear, accentuated by the unknown and the pervasive negativity on television. Second, there is learning. Eventually, they shed their needs to hoard supplies and come to grips with their personal emotions.

Finally, there is growth and a potential for marvelous opportunity. Kindness is being demonstrated abundantly. People are creating and sharing ways to stay physically fit, cook healthfully, and spend quality time with their families. Everyday heroes are becoming the norm. And excitingly, many are finding their purpose.

As a doctor of chiropractic and a functional medicine practitioner, my hope is that people will use this time to become increasingly mindful of their own health and wellness. This includes eating foods that support their immune system, exercising in order to create a more resilient body, and training the brain to adapt and grow through this experience. If this becomes habitual, it will help to reduce stress and improve overall health in the long term.

I work with patients to create a plan for each of them to thrive in these three key ways. However, there has been a critical missing component – their belief that they matter. If a patient is not emotionally ready or has unhealthy beliefs, no amount of information can help them move towards improved wellness. When my patients are free of negative self-concepts, their path towards a healthier lifestyle is infinitely easier.

Dr. Glasser and I have co-treated patients with overwhelming success keeping these principles at the forefront of our treatment missions. Our combined work has the immense power to be mentally, physically, and spiritually transformational. Instead of a fear-driven crisis, holistic wellness can be our "new normal."

Familial Units: Founded Upon Wellness and Love Based Relationships

Creating a family foundation to support su wellness requires healthy attraction to likely occur. A wholesome couple as a child's primary caregivers would fairly consistently demonstrate throughout the growing up years a truly loving and caring environment. The child who grew up observing spouses in constructive, affectionate, and, from what they can tell, even passionate involvement with each other has the edge. In other words, that child's home provides healthy memory imprints, healthy scenes like in a play but forever imprinted in their brains guiding their reactions soundlessly. Those imprints, not just as pictures, but as beliefs fostered, ever informs how to relate with one's spouse and one's children. These imprints as beliefs select one's mate. In a sense it's like a logarithm saying that's the 'one'.

Unhealthy attraction occurs in a similar manner with the exception that a child daily witnesses and observes ways of believing, thinking, valuing, behaving and feeling that fosters self-defeating patterns leading to unhappiness, unhealthy ways of being, unwholesome styles of functioning in a significant other relationship that lead to unhappiness.

Whether for better or for poorer outcome, it needs to be learned how to self-assess the actual sources of attraction. In one sense, it's no mystery. It's about seeking to re-create "home" whether that home is a nightmare or a lovely unit of existence.

Within any family generated, each spouse functions based upon the subconsciously held definitions witnessed as the couple grew up for each of these concepts: family, spouse, wife, husband, child, discipline/punishment, and religious or other values taught. Moreover, all of these affect attraction.

I love a line from the movie *Sleepless in Seattle* with Tom Hanks. The character he plays said so accurately something like: "Well I guess it was my subconscious mind and your subconscious mind that brought us together." No truer words could be spoken.

The relative quality or misery of marital outcome is based upon these sources of attraction and their definitions. Each familial unit develops accordingly over time. Are the sources healthy? Do the definitions produce joy or sadness, wellness or illness?

The Simplicity Conviction: A Wellness Summary

THE SIMPLICITY CONVICTION

The pledge: I am a Simplicity Conviction disciple dedicated to living its principles. My teachers are many. Their lessons enable a life lived lovingly with little pain and suffering to self or others.

THE PRINCIPLES OF THE SIMPLICITY CONVICTION

As a human being, on a humane journey, my commitment is to be guided by these convictions of common direction to be held as true but each available to higher truth.

1. Godliness — the goodness Energy wellspring within. Cultivating this loving Energy connects us each to the other in a fearless bond. See in hindsight the wise aspects of your direction.
2. Creating Heaven on Earth for all is the goal of life, a responsibility for each of us, each doing our part. Compassion/kindness/joy breathes life into life.

3. My mind-body is a Sanctuary requiring reverential care.
4. Wisdom, a life's quest, implies a thirst for learning and living truth's nuggets, and, not the least of these nuggets being the embrace of failure's lessons.
5. Success — the embrace, the honing and the exercise of each one's strengths for purposed service that brings one sustenance, as well as joy for self and others.
6. Pain can be of the moment. The extent of suffering is a matter of choice. Punishment/vengeance is the height of self and other destructive ignorance. Forgiveness and responsible reaction the antidote as we accept none as enemies or fundamentally evil rather as the perilous requiring adroit management.
7. Appropriately loving, affectionate and consistency of guidance, not pain, are far better engines for growth and change.
8. Love's archenemy is fear based living for it vomits angers' eruptions.
9. Responsible parenting requires a nurturing home in which a child's independence, farsightedness and the principles described herein are parentally exhibited and skillfully taught.
10. Humaneness primarily, and physiology secondarily, are to define female and male.
11. Quality life for all is sacred. Its skills require exemplary teaching at home and in society's institutions. Motivational teachers in public schools, starting from primary grades through college, need to provide broad-based learning, including civic duty, logic, ethics, the nature of truth and beauty, the essentialness of purposed vocations, and, what it means to love well are all essentials of home, community and school curriculum.
12. Integrity, becoming a lover of learning, the embrace of decency, an absence of violent comportment, plus success as defined above, when combined with authentic humbleness, indicate nobility. Grace is amazing. Grace is giftedness.

Under one banner we can unite as a
calm,
kindly and neighborly society
because for us:
Equally
All Lives Matter !

❄

Part 3

WELLNESS AS A WAY OF LIFE

12

Neighborhood Wellness Centers
THE COMMUNITY GARDENS OF THE 21ST
CENTURY

OUR WELLNESS IS about mind-body harmony. It's like the old song about love and marriage. In its "ideal" form:

"Love and marriage; they go together like a horse and
carriage; you can't have one without the other."

Sammy Cahn, lyrics; Jimmy Van Heusen, music.

Horses? Carriages? These images are pre-automobile — prehistoric, almost. Yet, I hope they serve to unite in our minds the concept of the essential, harmonious interdependency for the sake of overall well-being, also known as homeostasis.

A commitment to the body alone or to just the care of the mind, while better than nothing, won't provide the healthiness and joy in life that could otherwise be the case. In today's increasingly scientifically advanced world, we are learning the huge importance of brain-body interdependency for wellness. Nonetheless, it is fair to say that fixing the mind can also fix the body (see Chapter Eleven), just as fixing the body can fix the mind.

This chapter introduces you to the four basic ways to either fix or improve mind-body malfunction so it does not otherwise result in further pain and suffering. The helpful interdependency of these basic ways is important to appreciate. While I am not an expert in all of them, the fundamental ideas in this first area are important because they support the best outcomes for the fourth area, which is the arena of my expertise — the "Core Healing Way" elaborated upon in Part Two of this book.

While you likely have heard about aspects of at least two of these ways for advancing your brain-body wellness, I am discussing them all to introduce a concept that encourages a concerted effort for brain-body health. It's a dream I am about to share here, one that I have offered before at seminars conducted for my colleagues. It can reach fruition when You Matter quite a bit more than conglomerate medical facilities whose worship of the bottom line prevails and steals the resources for our wellbeing.

The Dream: Neighborhood Mind-Body Wellness Centers

While my dream may not sound new, I invite you to "hear," meaning to understand and constructively act on the whole of it. As we clear our heads from not just the current onslaught of news but also from the servitude to *the self-serving power structures that shape our society from top to bottom,* we will be better able to focus on eliminating what I call the "you don't matter virus," which has led up to and amplifies this horrible time.

As we climb out of this apocalyptic, deadly, and financially devastating juncture in our history, what ethical principle will guide our government, our world? This critical question dovetails my dream. It is the *You Matter Equally Ethic.* Grab hold of and hang on to that ethic for dear life because *it is for the quality of your dear life this book is written.*

Nations based on this ethic will consequently generate policies and budgets that prioritize the quality of your life along with the precious salvation of our Mother Earth. In other words, commanding our allegiance will be the healthful empowerment of us all *equally*. Allowing 'the golden calf worshiping' leaders to remain in power is voting for the truly crippled and quite pathologically ill supremacists who are destroying our quality of life and the death of our precious Mother Earth. They indifferently, and we often unwittingly, have created our vulnerability to deadly weapons of every form, from viruses to environmental catastrophes.

Mattering is the anti-virus for the world — not just for our nation. Actualizing our mattering equally and responsibly as a well-funded national policy will bring about my long-held passion to ease pain and suffering in this world. Out of that experience as to how this can happen, another dream was born. It is for your ease of accessing local, <u>multi-faceted wellness-fitness centers</u>.

These centers would use a host of proven ways to foster mind-body wellness as a way of life because each person can differ, holistically speaking. Presented here are some of the key ways that foster wellness development, support brain-body healing, wellness maintenance, and illness prevention.

I would *cherish* witnessing substantial seed money for creating a model mind-body wellness center — centers that could better serve the mental health needs of *all* our citizens who choose access. We all need wellness guidance that works rather than wastes money with band-aids, including programs aimed at our often ill-served veterans desperately in need of mind-body cures for post-traumatic stress disorder (PTSD). What a huge federal Veterans Affairs fortune would be saved. Veterans and their families would be ideally served in such local centers. (See Chapter Eight about curing PTSD using core healing.)

Moreover, these centers would not only offer mind-body wellness skill development opportunities but also prior to parenting decision-making trees. Am I — are we — ready to wholesomely parent? There's such an abundance of important considerations when it's the <u>child's</u> well-being that's primary.

Such centers would offer social and other wellness supportive skills and developmental activities for both children and adults, which is critical. Such centers would operate within a system that is *individualized*, a system that is tailored to each person walking through the door, so that each person has equal potential for an optimum wellness outcome *as a way of life*. Once birthed, my dream would be similar to the national altruism embodying the Peace Corps. The centers could be called something like: Mind-Body Wellness and Fitness Centers. Eventually, thousands of such wellness oriented, mind-body illness treatment and *prevention* centers would be located conveniently in each communities, maybe on school grounds.

Wellness orientation is financially smart. Such community-based wellness centers *would more than pay for themselves* by dramatically reducing medical and psychiatric treatment costs. The usefulness would be tracked. They could be associated with the nearest local university. Each relevant college within that university would be subcontracted to do continuing research and scientifically grow the cost effective offerings including the "ways" mentioned here. In addition, there would be mind-body wellness education classes, routine DNA testing for newcomers, prescriptive healthy and enjoyable eating plans, and also individually tailored physical fitness regimens.

Staffing Each Wellness Center

The staff for a wellness center would include such personnel as:

Intake specialist: Create an individualized, phased program for each community member entering the door based upon their goals and the services they need.

Psychiatrist: Medical emotional pain and behavioral management specialist. These professionals would also be titration specialists for appropriate supervision of anyone coming off meds. They would serve as a mind-body healer (Dabney Ewin, MD: 2009) and be a team leader for case management, and research. In addition, they would serve as a team consultant.

Psychiatric nurse: Medical protocol compliance coordinator, child development support counseling for parents, and mind-body core healer. A team consultant.

Clinical psychologist: Assessment services, as well as adult counseling supportive of the core healing concept. Develop and offer co-leadership to the team for elegant research design and responsible methodology with which to evaluate individuals' progress toward healthy goals plus their ability to form secure, kindness oriented relationships. Publish successes. A consultant. Neuropsychologist: Team with psychiatrist on behalf of clients. Assess extent of trauma. Provide appropriate treatment. Assist with research.

Psychotherapist: The primary core healer with expertise in cognitive behavioral therapy (CBT) (Burns, 1980/1999), TA, (Berne, 1964), inner child work (Riese, 1966 & Tyrell, 1977), plus other psychotherapeutic techniques acquired. A team consultant.

Marriage and family counselor: Wholesome family planning and systems development. A communication skills development specialist teaching reflective listening, for example. Overseeing educational programs for parents and children using the center's approved developmental program. Parent-effectiveness training that encourages taking the time to teach a child based on the consequences of their mistaken behavior rather than the expediency of punitive measures (Rudolph Dreikurs, 1968). In addition, counseling would address ways to "nurture your child's developing mind" (Siegel/Bryson, 2011), novel approaches to witnessing beauty (Rossi, 2012), and more. A team consultant at the center.

Social Worker: "Weave families into the fabric of their community." (David Brooks, 2019) The social worker would be uniquely qualified to: facilitate financial security for clients, f o r i n v o l v i n g t h e m i n planning for the health and welfare of themselves and their community including how to thwart threats to their community, one in which all thrive, are well informed and trained for success. Critically, a community goal would also be to foster compassionate, as well as service and wisdom oriented lives. This unique social worker leadership role encourages the "we" rather than the "us and them" type of humane community. Assimilation not ripping apart (ibid) should be fostered. (Check out the organization: Unite.) And, he/she also would serve as a team consultant.

Yoga/meditation instructor: Mind-body healer (van der Kolk, 2014). Team consultant.

Fitness instructor: Individualized virtual reality fitness regimen program developer.

Nutritionist: Expert in individualized wellness oriented eating programs for clients. Teaches nutrition classes.

Medical primary care type doctor: to help guide medical treatment referrals *or* when there is often the potential for psychogenic origin or contribution to body illness. A holistic care specialist!

Chaplain: This leader uses the "Simplicity Conviction" to bring people together spiritually who seek alternatives for spiritual connectedness. Fraught religious concepts need to be avoided.

Wellness entertainment programmer: An organizer who may, for instance, offer a movie night of wholesome, heartwarming films to watch; one who develops a center library for wellness oriented books that have been approved by the staff, other centers, and responded to well by the community.

Four Key Ways for Fixing the Brain-body at Such a Center

1. TALK THERAPY

Talk therapy, whether individual or group, serves many useful purposes.

• Clients need to be heard and not just simply "heard" but *under-stood* and then receive empathetic, helpful responses. Being understood is a huge thirst for millions. So many of my clients were raised as was I, with the familiar adage, "children should be seen but not heard." Think of the ways that phrase can be interpreted, can be defined. Such imprinted children grow into adults with beliefs that assure they select friends and / or lovers who do exactly that according to each's definition. They are seen but not heard.

How many marital fights echo, "but *you are not hearing* me," which means "you are not responding meaningfully nor doing what I need / want you to." After repetitions, such words are not just spoken with frustration, but with accumulating anger too.

Mistakenly, these folks are told they need to better communicate in order to fix that problem. While in a sense true, what they need first is core healing to change their identity to something like: All are not able but "I deserve to be heard, understood, and receive a thoughtful, though not necessarily, a compliant response."

• Talk therapy also teaches other useful skills and understandings, such as: how to live in the *now*. Why is living in the now important?

If one *lives in* the future, in a cloud of negative "what ifs," it becomes one way for "a worrier" to produce anxiety. On the other hand, when wise future planning and consequent decision-making is applied, then the selective use of "future think" is smart. That skill reduces anxiety because it is problem reduction and / or success oriented. When utilized, the outcome of this type of selective "future think" is anticipatory, risk assessing, and creative. Such wise decision making orientation reduces anxiety. It is not the repetitive "what ifs" and the rehashing required to fulfill being a "worrier."

If one lives in the past, in their regrets, it is one way to generate depression. If you decide you don't want to "depress," then the choice, the likely identity you are choosing alternatively, is to do "joy," and to "live with an attitude of gratitude" (Oprah's words of wisdom). Remember, 'depressing' can very much be a choice.

Also, focusing instead in the now fosters stress reduction. It's a relief from the overload of future thought and the exhaustion of past regrets. It's a setting aside of one's long, long to-do list and one's long, long worry list, and more efficiently and entertainingly utilizes one's time in the now. But don't misunderstand. Future *planning and learning from ones past* has its place.

• Talk therapy can help develop communication skills such as non-judgmental, reflective listening. It ties together with empathy and compassion skill development.

• Developing the talk therapy skills of being solution oriented when "concerns" arise helps to eliminate the energy sapping rehashing of worry. Learned worrying style has the requisite identity, "I am a worrier" or worse yet, "I worry about everything."

Parents are particularly vulnerable to the concept of being 'worriers.' In part, our society accepts it as a definition of being a "good" parent. From my experience as a hypno-analyst that conviction, that aspect of definition for being a worrier parent needs deleting.
Replacing it would like: I am solution oriented. And, I don't waste my time being a worrier in order to keep my children safe and cared for. My job as a parent is modeling plus teaching a how to be safe solution/action orientation. That approach is stress reducing. Worrying is stress creating for all concerned. Stress, as you well know, is unhealthy.

Remember being a worrier requires repetitive, mind-overloading negative thinking. Self-concepts and beliefs generative of negative thoughts produces increasing amounts of stress. It's the go-nowhere worrying style. It is the *learned, blotted up, mind imprinted style, which is absorbed through familial beliefs' exemplification.*

Allowing yourself to be a "worrier" robs you of the rejuvenating effects of sleep. Thoughts generated to help you worry keep you awake. Such loss carries the risk of illness development, grouchiness, the common cold, and the pain of weariness.

Worrying *seems* to come naturally. Actually, worrying and what to worry about is *learned* from one or more of our parents and/or their parents (our grandparents) and on back throughout human history.

People tend to take worrying for granted and make the mistake of brushing it off as that is what love is about. While it looks like and is reinforced like a "habit," being a worrier first and foremost is a self-concept, *an identity implemented according to the definitions* for it we witness as children.

Alternative identity formation would help avoid this "worry" potential and its amplification over time. When core healing, the replacement I use after deleting "worrier" as mentioned earlier is, "I am solution-oriented as a *concern* arises." The word "concern" as the replacement doesn't have the "loaded" meanings in the concept of being a worrier.

In addition, talk therapy can help teach that being cautious is genetic. It helps us survive, which of course is our prime directive. However, worry was mistakenly birthed from caution by over-doing it as if more is better.

Unfortunately, caution has morphed into dangerous identity development not just as a worrier but also as being shy. I'd rather my child be taught:

- When and how to be cautious.
- How to have an eye for and an appropriate response to various forms of danger.
- How to know whom to trust.
- Managing when mistaken about who to trust.
- How to be safe and sociable.

These lessons as alternatives to shy and worrier identities would significantly reduce alcohol, cannabis, and drug misuse.

• Talk therapy is a form of teaching. Individual or group classes/sessions can be very helpful to teach what is taught here and from other resources. After all, wellness is akin to the old three R's [reading, writing, and arithmetic] and to the STEM (science, technology, engineering, and math) programs *but it is far more important.*

I used to be a schoolteacher and a school principal helping shepherd the children that teachers didn't know how to deal with. *Teaching a child who is well is far easier than teaching one who is ill.* However, illness is definitely changeable, especially with unconditionally caring, loving, structured and informed guidance. The earlier addressed, the better.

• Then there's talk therapy with an experienced and intuitive therapist who can generate with the client an epiphany — that "aha!" moment sparking brain-rewiring opportunities. An epiphany is a kind of "light bulb" surprise moment. In that fraction of a moment, one's identity can be profoundly changed for the better as one's truth to a problem is caused to evidence itself.

• Talk therapy is important to use for introductory instruction necessary to prep an adult for core healing. A flavor of some of that prep "stuff" is above. Then there's the 'nitty-gritty' preparedness for life "stuff."

2. MEDITATION SKILL DEVELOPMENT (as written by: Cameron Estes)

Ancient practices of meditation have been used to help improve the mind/brain health by small groups through the ages. The more recent Western focus on mindfulness has given a different slant to many practices. Meditation has been used to calm one's mind and to help develop focus; the mindful practices tend to emphasize the present moment with intention and clarity. These practices develop a heightened awareness of the thoughts and how and if we are participating with those thoughts.

One practice that can create a different relationship for us employs mindful meditation — being a witness to the thoughts, emotions, and beliefs that come into our awareness. Being more aware of that which is transpiring in the mental formations of our brain activity allows us to be calmer and more present.

The ancients said that our thoughts could do one of two things:

Create hell in our life.

Create a heaven in our life.

Dr. Glasser would say that our beliefs create our thoughts' direction. She would concur that learning to manage our thoughts empowers our better governance as it creates supportive beliefs.

Being possessed by our own thoughts is the usual condition of most people unless they practice taking a pause when dealing with their thoughts. The "constant monologue" of our mind talk keeps us distracted and mired in thoughts that have little to do with the present moment.

The best way to describe the benefits from a meditation practice is to describe my own experience that started eighteen years ago. Everyone will have their own experience with attempts to begin a meditation practice, but the first lesson I learned was to build upon what appeared to be positives.

Meditation for me began after reading a book by Eckhardt Tolle wherein he stated that there were a thousand forms of meditation. He suggested one that I interpreted as a focus on the inside of my hand. I discovered that by trying to focus on the inside of my hand, I relaxed and was not lost in the constant thoughts that were plaguing me at that time. Those thoughts I called the "woulda, shoulda, couldas." They were obsessive and rarely silent. Focusing on my hand silenced them briefly. It was a pleasant enough change that I tried doing it more often. I knew through experience that I could not shut my thoughts down, but a focus briefly on something else did have a calming effect. The inside of my hand worked for several weeks. I turned to my hand whenever I remembered to stop the insistent thoughts.

I soon discovered that focusing on my breath worked just as well and did not require the focus I seemed to require for hand meditation. My life was rapidly calming down and I was finding daily life more comfortable.

I had the opportunity to tour a residential home for abused women. My immediate thought was that these women could use a meditation program since I imagined that their minds must be filled with "woulda, coulda, shoulda." The nun who ran this facility liked my suggestion of a meditation program but did not want any "people with saffron robes." This comment sent me on a research trip for some practice that might not be too Buddhist oriented.

The search led me to a program developed in England that had been started by Jon Kabat Zinn and Oxford University for students having problems. The results were very positive. From there, I followed up with Kabat Zinn's MBSR program. MBSR stands for Mindfulness Based Stress Reduction, which Zinn had created first for cancer patients and then caregivers at the University of Massachusetts. I got a set of compact discs for the program, which combined light yoga with meditation. The merger of the mind-body awareness was intense. It did require a real commitment to follow the program, but I wanted something I could offer the abused women. They were my catalyst and encouragement. By the time I had finished the eight-week program, I was aware that I was different. My reactive nature was vastly slowed, my ability to identify what was happening in my mind and body was greatly enhanced, my understanding of my thought processes had changed, and I was much more comfortable in my daily living.

I was no longer at war with myself or the world around me. My mind life had not become heaven, but it had certainly become more enjoyable. I really had an understanding of living in the present moment.

I found some women who had the MBSR training and who were willing to volunteer by starting the meditation program at the home for abused women. It quickly changed to just me and a wonderful volunteer named Sheila, who would work with ladies one morning a week. They connected quickly with the yoga side of our presentation while the mindfulness took time.

Combining yoga and mindfulness helps the practitioner realize the unity there of mind/body. The discomfort one feels in one's body can soon be looked at differently when practicing mindful meditation. The nature of the thoughts that arise out of a feeling of discomfort can be seen differently as one recognizes the occurrence of pain and then the mind activity to revisit that site of pain. Slowly the women began to recognize that there was some truth for them in the idea that pain is inevitable, but the suffering is optional.

Our classes evolved over time from complaint sessions about body pains, children problems, abuser problems, to how they were moving through their lives, reaching their kids, feeding them, walking, talking, being more honest with their feelings, and recognizing their emotions.

The best moments occurred when one of the ladies described being in court with her abuser and shared how she remembered to turn away and just breathe for a few minutes. She could then return to their discussion with clarity and less emotionality.

During these times of working with the abused women, I developed a severe arthritic hip situation. I found that the yoga of the classes helped, so I went for physical therapy, which helped for a number of years. I was able to hike and travel for several years until the arthritis progressed to such an extent that surgery was required. The mindful meditation allowed me to deal with pains and my life in a manner that would never have been possible previously.

Learning to live in the present moment is not easy. Everything in our society and training seems to work against that idea. Meditation requires practice, but there is not much that is worthwhile in life that does not require repetition to hone skills. Experiencing the present moment in a mindful or aware state is awesome.

Can knowledge and personal experiences with meditation enrich our self-understanding? That is certainly one of the doors being opened here for you to consider seriously. With meditation, there are several healthful benefits all worthy of appreciation and justify its inclusion in wellness centers.

Control over runaway thoughts is another important part of the training involved. Over time, the beliefs generating the discomforting assault of runaway thinking begin undergoing a shift. From a core healing perspective, the causative beliefs to those discomforting thoughts were being rewritten with such alternative direction, with such practice.

Practicing meditation teaches us to be in control by employing a skill set that shifts the nature of the beliefs. Over time, rewiring of the brain occurs. There is an eventual shift to better beliefs and the deletion of the originating beliefs. That is what allows for better thought control. *Depression and anxiety diminish as one's sense of control increases.* As stress reduces, bodily inflammation subsides. As inflammatory processes are reduced, one's immune system can strengthen. In other words, meditation each day is a very healthy practice.

Abundant research demonstrates so many wonderful mind-body benefits from the practice. It is a *must* for community wellness centers to offer and, of course, to teach.

3. MEDICALLY (Neurofeedback, Epigenetics, Medication: Psyche Meds)

A. Neurofeedback- (D. Corydon Hammond, Ph.D., Journal of Neurotherapy, 2011)

Since early 1960, with the advent of "alpha" brain training, wonderful advances have occurred in the arena of brain-body functional health, giving credence to "brainwave training." This is called EEG biofeedback or neurofeedback. Specially trained medical and mental health professionals like Cory Hammond, Ph.D., in Salt Lake City, Utah, and Steve Warner, Ph.D. in Central Florida, utilize this technology in wonderful ways.

Neurofeedback is not a "do-it-yourself project." It is a mind-body technology based upon training the brain to regulate and balance its component structures. For example, when the midline of the cerebral cortex has too much fast wave energy (high beta activity generally used for thinking and mental processing), it can lead to obsessive worry, anxiety and hyper-vigilance. With a qEEG analysis, we "listen in" to brain activity with electrodes (much the way a sensor records heart rate activity) for several minutes and then compare the acquired "raw waves" to a normative database. This allows us to determine which waves at what locations are under-powered or too aroused.

It's like a brain road map that provides clinicians the information to develop interventions. The interventions may be as simple as placing a sensor on the scalp over an area that corresponds with excitable activity. By rewarding the brain to calm that area, the person starts to feel more relaxed. This occurs as the person watches a movie, and when the movie plays brightly, it's a signal (learning theory) to the brain that this is the right direction — either lowering the activation or increasing it.

Neurofeedback has been researched for many years producing thousands of research articles. There are several national and international professional groups that promote and train professionals in the use of neurofeedback techniques.

Because neurofeedback has excellent credentials for brain-body helping and/or healing a host of conditions, it's the type of opportunity my dream neighborhood center would definitely offer to the appropriate candidates based upon a qEEG evaluation.

Why? Here is a partial list of what neurofeedback can potentially improve, if not entirely resolve:

- ADD/ADHD (attention deficit disorder and attention deficit hyperactivity disorder)
- anxiety problems
- obsessive compulsive issues
- learning disabilities
- autism
- depression
- stroke
- epilepsy
- dementia and many other issues

B. Epigenetics

Here's Merriam-Webster's definition for Epigenetics:

"...the study of heritable changes in gene function that do not involve changes in DNA sequence." Actually, it is more than that. It's about the activation *and* the deactivation of negative gene functioning. One could read what was just said, shrug their shoulders and say: "What's the big deal?" Or, just plain, "so what?" I ask that you cast that reaction aside until you hear this true story.

A woman came to me for core healing for a variety of issues. Her primary issue was that her oncologist at a prestigious hospital had given her one year to live in the best case scenario, because a rare form of genetically caused cancer was destroying her body.

How does epigenetics become relevant in this grave situation? To help get the picture, I suggest this. Imagine an on/off light switch to an attic. Now, imagine that the light switch has been off for years. There was no particular need to go up there and especially not at night.

It is now in the "on" position due to an unknown event. Genetically speaking, up until that exact point in time, the switch was in the "off" position. In our illustrative example, a neighbor tells you there's a light on in the attic every night for about a week. That's unusual. So, you go to check it out.

The woman, dealing with an unusual physical symptom, went to get it checked out with her doctor. After much testing she was diagnosed with the onset of a rare cancer due to her genetic coding.

For some reason, at a precise moment in her life, the "on" switch activated the cancer problem. Remember, the prospect for cancer had been there all her life. Hmmmm, so precisely, why *then* did it activate? After all, that DNA sequencing was something she was born with.

But when it did turn "on," the symptomatology associated with improper cell regeneration took off. Now, you are invited to imagine what happened. With core healing that gene was returned to the "off" position. In this instance, the DNA sequencing was not changed. She was and to this day still is diagnosable with a blastoid variant of lymphoma and a very "aggressive type." BUT, this unhealthy, life-threatening activation had been returned to the "off" position with core healing. The answer to why the switch went on then, why the cancer manifested at that point in time though there all her life, became the answer to what belief needed changing. Based on the truth, I was enabled to rewire and reprogram her in such a way that, epigenetically, her switch was turned "off." So, while still diagnosed with that type of cancer, there's been no negative symptomatology and no death. That was five years ago.

Can I definitively say I cured her cancer? *Absolutely not.* It has recently returned. The question is "why again"? Why now? Continuing "elegant" research at each neighborhood's mind-body wellness and fitness centers can assist with relevant data collected with which to foster not only a consistency of "best practice" approaches but possibly provide data under such circumstance to help return the cancer to the "off" position again.

C. <u>Medication (Psychotropic)</u>

Psychotropic medication manages symptomatology. It *does not cure* but helps to control emotional and behavioral problems resulting from negative self-concepts and beliefs that are generated in traumatic situations. Some have treacherous side effects requiring very close monitoring.

On the flip side, medications' benefits include buying time for the pain of a trauma to subside. During that healing time, patients may utilize potential supportive, sometimes curative, measures such as prescribed "talk therapy" or an often "better yet" for more thorough resolution: a core healing Rx.

Medications are also good at improving functionality for those with schizophrenia, bipolar disorder, significant depression and/or anxiety.

D. <u>Medication (Psychogenic)</u>

Medications have been relied on for making one feel better or curing a physical problem. Definitely, they have earned their place. Some work curatively, some partially. As empirical support grows for the use of clinical hypnosis, one arena of success *medically* is with what are now called brain-gut interaction disorders such as IBS. One gentleman I worked with decades ago had severe IBS. The medications prescribed weren't working. He was frantic. With Core Healing hypnotherapy, we got it 90% better. Heal the mind the body follows. But don't forget, medications can support the journey.

4. The Core Healing, Client-Centered Way

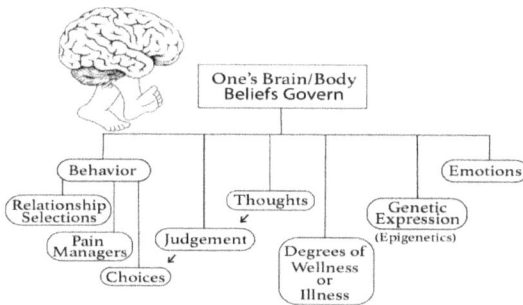

One's Brain/Body
Beliefs Govern

Behavior — Emotions

Relationship Selections — Thoughts — Genetic Expression

Pain Managers — Judgement — (Epigenetics)

Choices — Degrees of Wellness or Illness

This paradigm is essential to understanding if you want the potential for total mind-body wellness as a way of life. Your makeup is governed by your genes, your sex (along with their attendant hormones), your drive to survive and by your beliefs that begin developing early.

Your beliefs reign. Beliefs are what generate your feelings, your thoughts, etc. (See diagram above.) They start, pause, accelerate or decelerate your reactions. They govern epigenetically. They govern you amorally for better or worse.

Madison Avenue types (savvy marketers), dictators, conspiracy peddlers, tabloid news vendors (newspaper, Internet, Cable 'news' and radio), money driven religious leaders, self-serving politicians, etc. all understand that controlling you means offering you salvation from the primal fears they stirred within you. It is mental illness developing at it's most despicable. Cruelty and death abide.

Core Healers are interested in your having self-control in the ways you want to become. Core Healers take you on an into self, truth seeking journey to accomplish your goals for improving your well being. It is what is called a client-centered approach.

Psycho-therapeutically, "client-centered" is more effective than "therapist-centered". Remember, the truths being sought to help resolve a client's issues are within the client and seldom in the experienced mind of a talk NLP therapist. With the truth seeking of the word "why", it is far speedier to go directly into the brain-body source of the client utilizing hypno-analytics to seek out, delete and replace the beliefs causing their problems.

Here are some typical examples of "why" questions that clients present for therapy:

- Why don't I feel any love for myself?
- Why do I feel so anxious when I wake in the morning?
- Why do I believe I shouldn't exist?
- Why am I so depressed?
- Why have I wound up divorced and marry the same type of guy again and again with the same "M.O."
- Why do I feel like such a failure?
- Why don't I feel like I want to live anymore?

As an aside, these adult "whys" remind me of the maturity difference as to how a child speaks their "whys." A little child might sound even a bit whiny like. . . ."Why daddy," "Why mommy?" This question is often followed by a parental response of, "Because I told you so" or "Because I told you to." Then the child might ask, "Do I 'haveta'?" Eventually, children may then say to themselves: "*don't bother asking 'why' anymore.*" And thus, another negative self-concept and belief is born.

The reason I am sharing this little aside is that how a parent handles this sort of typical situation, in no small way becomes illness or wellness developing of the inquisitive child. Curiosity is one of our inborn survival tools, one that I see as a gift when nourished. But, in illness development style, and compounding the accumulation of negative beliefs, when the parent can be heard to say: "Because I said so, that's why," as the father unbuckles his belt to emphasize his authority to punish if the child doesn't do as he/she is told, fosters a belief like: don't question.

Though perhaps rebellious at times, will the child become a rebel as retaliation or will that child become obedient and unquestioning of an authority figure who punishes with whimsy for lack of obedience in carrying out orders? Has the foundation been laid for Nazi-type obedience or similarly to a demanding boss figure?

On the other hand, the wellness approach is *when parents take the time* to educate the child on the why and the when of absolute obedience as a must so the parent can keep the child safe until he or she can do so on his or her own. This way, the child can be guided to become compliant due to preparation of circumstance when the immediate, obedient/safe response is called for, especially in an emergency.

When the situation is not life threatening, parents can use the time to teach. Teachable moments present themselves. It is a great opportunity to answer the child's "why" and help shape their critical thinking, logical thinking, and problem solving skills.

Remember, wellness reflects persuasion as in using these teachable moments to find meaningful alternatives that make sense to the child. Compliance from the child's point of view becomes: I do it because I want to. That creates lasting constructive change with little or no supervision.

Compliance that requires threat for adherence reflects compulsion. It is that "do it or else" warning. In that scenario, the parent is then assuming the enforcer role and the child becomes someone who requires an enforcer whether that person be a wife, a boss, or some other form of "gatekeeper."

Core healing is about the *persuasiveness* of hearing one's own sought-out truth, in one's very own words and especially when the words of that truth come out of one's own mouth. It transports one, instantaneously, from an illness position on that issue to one of wellness. A better, more mature belief can now govern because it's the issue the client asked help to correct. *Their choice to be better in that particular way was then freed, was empowered to happen and to be actualized.*

Funding Public Wellness Centers

These neighborhood mind-body fitness centers need to be classi-
fied as a public service. In a sense, I see these centers as both
economic and yet as a kind of concierge service meaning only the
best for you.

It's lovely to have wonderful ideas, but there is always a BUT that
arises. In this case, how can we afford them? My answer is "how
can we not?" Wellness orientation is cheaper in the long run. The
wealthy, because they can spend a fortune on receiving the best
that health care offers, live longer and healthier lives. But a fortune
doesn't have to be spent, per person, if done right in the first place,
e.g., when hospitals don't become thieving conglomerates.

Therefore, it is reasonable to ask how can we foot the bill? What is
fair? Who should pay for these desperately needed centers for
wellness? Stop the thieving and a huge pile of money appears. We
the people should be held accountable too. Other sources to
consider to create wellness centers' funding reservoir can be from
NIMH (National Institute for Mental Health). Yet other sources:

- fossil fuel industries taxed for the wellness centers
- transfer of federal funding subsidies from oil and gas
  industries to NIMH
- taxes on carbon emissions
- taxes on gun owners who have "warring" weaponry, ghost
  guns, gun magazines
- taxes on gun shops, gun shows, etc.
- parents who do not have their firearms secured from their
  children
- the military industrial complex
- hate speech sources. (They make a fortune off of us.)
- tobacco/vaping industries

In addition to these "just" sources, there are two other sources to consider: a combination of private philanthropy and partnership with public funding.

Initially, enough money would be used to set up a model center in the next year or two. There has to be a leadership team specifically tasked with making logical coalitions happen.

From a governmental standpoint, substantial additional health funding can be reallocated from Medicare, Medicaid, and from Veterans Benefits Administration including their mental health budgets. These funds can then be allocated based upon each neighborhood's percentage of groups served: seniors, veterans, soldiers' families, lower income folks, those imprisoned at home, etc.

Redirecting a portion of the money spent on prison incarceration, particularly as we enter an era of rethinking how we house inmates with ever-improving technologies to monitor at home incarcerations makes good sense. Lowering recidivism isn't the goal for privatized prisons. Making money is. Simple mathematics: the more prisoners the more the profit, the greater the waste of tax dollars, and worst of all the misery, the tragedy of wasted lives.

In addition, creating hospital and college affiliations makes sense. Also, Wellness Centers could be located on military bases. This latter idea would allow for PTSD prevention programs to be researched and developed. Regarding private philanthropy, uniting in common cause to eliminate overlapping services is wise.

Yes, the centers cost money for governments now stretched thin. But few things beyond survival itself could be more important than bestowing our society with the tools to become whole again. Support to ensure our future generations live lives of mattering equally and kindly, lives rich with self and other respect is essential. The question is how are we going to help those who believe they don't matter, a self deemed worthless.

It's like a third or more of our population is on a 'kamikaze' type mission to deliberately commit suicide in the effort of killing the ill-perceived, so-called enemy. Those who feel inferior act superior to go from powerlessness to powerful. It's dangerous.

The cost of ignoring our public, collective needs is exponential. Constant health threats, racial divides, greed and a barrage of demeaning messages overpower our mothers, fathers, sons and daughters. For centuries we have looked to churches and nonprofits to lift us up. Now it is time for our elected leaders to put into place a systematic plan, a plan that is the antidote to the gross failure orientation of authoritarian, self-serving supremacists.

Let us invest in places that both lift us up and give us a promise for tomorrow's tomorrow. Save you. Save your children. Save the planet. It's true. This type of loving commitment offers extraordinary opportunity. Heal ourselves. Heal our children. Heal the World.

These are the most critical self identities to be operationalized by the mind-body as they are anti-anxiety, anti-depression, anti-addiction, anti-suicide and as a plus, pro-social identities worth cultivating.

I am a person who is..........

A

Appreciative, as in having the ability to express meaningfully what I am grateful for.

Attentive due to having the ability to, and wanting/able to listen reflectively with comprehension and sensitivity.

B

Beauty appreciative realizing the beauty in the appearance of a kindness oriented being. (Unkind beings look ugly, even fierce.)

Balanced, living a life that includes wholesome fun, gets quality/adequate sleep, works out, makes time for quality relationships and has a commitment to an integrity approach to work and money management/savings.

(*Doing their*) Best. Life isn't fun nor healthy driven by extreme perfectionism (BPD results leading to escapism [as in delusions] and exhaustion [as in depression used to escape and recuperate].

C

Caring: caring about self and others.

Compassionate, utilizing the skill of exercising *empathy*, gentleness and diplomacy through comprehending the other's context.

Civic minded, participating in identifying, discussing and resolving community and national issues. The goal: building a sense of harmonious direction and then working toward consensus for resolution.

Considerate due to the ability to be thoughtful about what the other person may need/want, too.

D

Decisive rather than wishy-washy when exercising pro/con assessment skills that sooner or later arrive at the point for resolution.

Decent, as in being moral, polite and gracious.

E

Excellence oriented. Excellent, top notch performance is understood to be a better direction versus perfection.

Empathic as in having the ability to appreciate why people different than self could be acting as they do.

Equal. Life isn't about competing but rather strength sharing.

Ethical. Becoming governed by wellness principles and forethought.

(*Embraces self-chosen and administered*) Euthanasia for those 75 and older and/or are in intractable pain and/or not able to live much longer. Rules that are as gentle and kind for humans as for our pets. It is humane. (The "meek" must prevail.)

F

Fit: being mentally/physically fit, creating a mind/body that supports a healthy life.

Forgiving. I strive to let go of pain and anger and avoid vengeance.

Friendly.

Forgiving: able to rapidly let go of pain and anger.

G

Gentle.

Good and good enough in any given moment as a person doing their best.

Grace appreciative meaning acting with compassionate dignity.

H

Heroism: living and leading with the courage to act consistently with decency kindness, integrity and creativity to fulfill the conviction that healthy life and love are worth gifting one's life energy to accomplish.

Harmonious: When we disagree, it is how we resolve differences or even maintain our differences of approach with dignity.

Humanomics defining so as to be an improvement on crony capitalism and greed that results from the unmanly aspiring to be the richest and most revered. (Underneath, their identity is a loser.)

I

Independent, yet able to be a team player.

J

Joyful.

K

Kind: with self and others.

L

Learned having developed a love of learning.

Loving of others and wholesomely of self.

M

Matters. Every human is granted gifts and talents that when encouraged and developed allow the individual to live a purposed life sharing their gifts because they are taught: "sharing is caring," "caring is sharing." (Madeline Sherak)

N

(Able to say) No and mean it.

Non-violent; non-punitive.

O

Open. Has the ability to be appropriately vulnerable. There is nothing shameful about imperfections. Hiding them doesn't allow me to outgrow them. Being open allows for love to venture in.

P

Problem-solving.
Playful.

Purposed.

Q

Quiet. I enjoy the ability to just be silent, to be nourished by and to appreciate quiet.

R

Responsible, has accountability.

Resilient. I have the ability to bounce back using problem-solving and/or a sense of humor when I make dumb mistakes or take an incorrect direction.

Respectful: of self, others and knowledge.
(does) Right by self and others which is different than having to be right.

S

Spiritual, one who is able to share loving Energy that is life Eternal.

Service oriented to my community, country, and World.

Sportsmanship oriented.

Strong: one who nurtures and constructively uses their strengths.

(a) Steward providing loving guidance, creating the conditions for all life to thrive by being responsible for the care and guidance of one's children, one's home, one's neighborhood, and the overall well-being of all life.

T

Thoughtful
Thankful.
Truthful/Truth seeking.

U

Unconditionally loving: versus "I'll love you if."

V

(*Enjoys*) Victory but not cheating to get it.

W

Wisdom: quest for wisdom as a way of life. (The Simplicity Conviction)

X…is for hugs and xxxx (s).

Y

Youthful: maintaining a youthful persona, a young style of being.

Glossary B

Illness Developing Beliefs

I am a person who is ....

A

Apocalyptic. One who invites end of days disaster. "Be careful what you wish for". Together you might succeed. Living a wellness path is much smarter, much more fun and a lot safer.

Attitude oriented: "having a sneering attitude."

Abandoning: believing you must deserve to be abandoned by self, others, and God.

Arrogant: raised with a fundamental sense of inadequacy, entitlement and/or superiority.

B

Bad: even seeing self as evil.

Bossy.

Bored: acting bored rather than engaged by mattering based on one's strengths.

Bullying.

C

Controlling: being controlling of everything, others, situations, money, children, etc.

Cheat: one who steals from another.

Continuously Competitive

Controlling without the consent of those controlled.

Cruel: uses hurting others to release one's own pain.

Cynical: choosing to be a sore loser versus proudly building upon one's failures and the roadblocks of life.

D

Dependent. Or, "acts" dependent or is unskilled for independent life.
Dictatorial.
Dumb: rather than human. (None of us know it all.)

Dynastic: centralizes power around self, the "only I matter position".

E

Entitled: only I and mine matter.
Exploitative: taking advantage of others.
Exclusive: excluding those defined as inferior and/or the other.

F

(a)Failure.
Fear-filled.

G

Gauche: vulgar and tasteless.
Greedy: money accumulation for status and power.
Godless: lacks loving Energy connectivity with others.

H

Hateful. ('Vomits' all over others as a fear based shield.)

Hopelessness: unskilled in living on the platform of hope.

Hypocrite. Untrustworthy.

I

Ignorant. Lives life generally bored gypped of the joy of learning.

Inadequate. Believes self to be ill equipped anatomically, intellectually, and / or fundamentally.

Indecisive: the hallmark of an extreme perfectionist. One who lacks critical thinking and problem resolution skills.

Irresponsible: scared to be at fault and / or punished. Also, unskilled in utilizing mistakes.

J

Just joking: jokingly / hurtfully poking fun at someone.

Jealous. The ugly art of living in envy. Fear of unlovability.

K

Killer. One who murders others without remorse. (There can be the day that together we will have created a compassionate mindset that makes being a killer, for any reason, a thing of the past.)

L

Loser. Seeing yourself as never able to win and therefore sets it up to ultimarely lose.

Liar. One who escapes their reality&truth about self, others and life.

Libertarian. A supremacist favoring an Ayn Rand 'dog eat dog' type world where government is bad.

M

Magical thinker. One who sits back and awaits salvation. Malicious.

Enjoys causing pain.

Money monger. Accumulates money to feel god-like power and control over others. Being rich to gain attention and / or inclusion.

N

Negativity oriented. Delights in fear and chaos engendering.
Believes others are not good enough (in some way or ways) and
certainly not equal to self.

O

Oppressive: stifling creativity and joy.

Other-controlling.

P

Powerless.
Power hungry. Feels inferior in some critical way or ways and
desperately needs to feel superior.
Purposeless.
Punishing: most especially of self, let alone one's child and others.
Perfectionist: unrelentingly driven to make no mistakes.
Proving worth: having to prove yourself as good enough.
Proselytizing: convert or else.

Q

Quitter: being a quitter is one hallmark of a loser.

R

Rages. Uses anger to intimidate. Is fear based. Anger is a cover-up.

Rapes: Physically violates the person-hood of another as pent-up
fears' release. Vengeance seeking.

Repressive.

Ridicules. Belittles another to raise oneself up.

S

Sickly. See self as sickly even when not.

Selfish. Solely about self (negative v positive selfish).̄

Self-righteous. Puritanical in style about a cause!

T

Thief.

Tyrannical. Authoritarian and dictatorial.

U

Unfeeling: not empathetic.

Unlovable: and acts to make it so.

Under-educated: lacking information and truth-seeking skills.

V

Victim. Unwittingly plays out that identity usually with pathos.

Vengeful. Acts as a huge danger to human and earthly survival. (Forgiveness that fosters empathy is far more gratifying, healthful and does real justice for all concerned.)

Violent. It's the learned behavior of a poorly raised person.

W

Warrior: one who embraces combat/fighting whether for the sake of being *powerfully* rich, an imperialist or for seeming like a hero as in someone who matters. (There are no "good" wars. None. They are provoked. To say there are Spiritual warriors is antithetical. Moreover, wholesome *parenting is usually and severely compromised* by those trained to be warriors: those trained to be violent, to kill, plus those taught to know the 'ins and outs' of how to 'make a killing'. They often turn a 'blind eye' to warring's cruelty.)

Worrier: a being who thinks negatively plus exaggerates threat.

Weak. A person who sees oneself as spineless and/or not strong enough. Worthless.

Y

Yeller: one who believes they don't deserve to be heard or one who acts to over-power another.

Of the conditions below, what percent of each of these is due to the type of reasons that are known as psychogenic. These were discovered due to the use of Core Healing.

Anorexia: A little 10 year old girl physically developing but wanting to maintain her body as that of a boy. (Full story on page 146)

Asthma: Not enough love to breath in.

Bi-Polar Disorder: This condition results from failing, and, steep self disappointment of not being perfect enough. Also, research that depression might well be for secondary gain to allow oneself to rest after expending so much effort that they are in a state of exhaustion.

Bulimia: Two sources to look into... too fat to be attractive (wind up alone and/or abandoned)... fear of being unlovable.

Cancer: Self punishment... especially for deeming self as having failed their child(ren) in a significant way.

IBS: (Irritable Bowel Syndrome) = That part of a body one's belief(s) selects as the depository, the warehouse of anxiety. Others include: neck; shoulders; heart (the mitral valve is particularly effected as a result); etc.

Lower Back Pain: (see John Sarno's book Healing Back Pain. 1991)

Migraines: A way to escape responsibility or something you very much need a break from doing. (They also carry a flavor of finding oneself <u>not good enough</u> in a consequential way.)

Obesity: Modeled behavior plus operationalizing an assumption of genetic predisposition.

Suicide: Escape from the pain of conviction about self as not mattering or only mattering if dead. (See page 146)

Acknowledgments

In one sense, some would say there is no originality. As a perpetual student, I am but sharing here what I learned from others. That part is true. Be that as it may, what I do see as an original contribution is the *targeting of the key source of the world's malaise*. It revolves around the major increase of more and more of us not mattering equally. While equality is known as wise, it is little practiced. However, quite literally, "mattering" equally/kindly is a life/death, mind-body wellness perspective essential to embrace at this very pivotal moment in time for survival to lastingly have a chance. It is no exaggeration to say everyone's existence depends upon it.

The people listed below have been key helpers, each in their own way supporting this book's messaging to you. I am their student, a grateful receiver of their guidance and of their support. In alphabetical order they are:

Lil Barcaski: She helped me organize this book.

Mary Ann Barefield: For her courageous, dedicated and 'techy' help.

Kimberly Besuden: DC: A true healer. See her article's contribution.

Laurean Crowley: Copy editing.

Cameron Estes: For his personal sharing regarding his journey into meditation first as a student and from there, over time, as a knowledgeable volunteer teacher in after school programs.

Julie Fletcher: Photographer.

Charles Frishman: A man who is a model of kindly mattering. He's been a major help in improving this effort, this book, on behalf of humanity's wellness living.

Google: What a marvelous, helpful resource.

Mark Hastings: For cheering me forward on this labor of love to promote the idea *from human to humane evolutionary direction* based upon my lessons gleaned from being a core healer.

Mary Frances Hauser: High school friend and benefactor. She was my first donor, helping me to afford taking this time *to promote kindness as the overarching manner for how we choose to matter.* The better we do kind "mattering" with self and others, the more wellness-prone and the better at loving we are. Mary was kindness personified from when I first met her all those years ago.

Jesse Kunerth: For cover illustration.

Michelle and Mike Krueger: The kind pillars that a writer like me leans upon.

Nicole Reid: A behind the scenes heroine for advancing this cause.

Donald J. Tyrell, Ph.D.: My therapist from my mid-thirties who guided my healing journey. And, quite critically, he left a healer's imprints that I effectively replicate when Core Healing. His style of inner child work re-birthed is so powerfully effective.

Eileen Van Den Berg: A gardener of the soul.

Steve Warner, Ph.D.: A supportive, distinguished colleague who helped with this book's sharing about the importance of neurofeed-back. Steve also helped with my last book about Core Healing. Though that book is now outdated, the stories it relates are as true today as the day they were written.

About the Author

Dr. Joyce Fern Glasser

A unique self-concept imprinted in her mind by her father, this book by Dr. Joyce Glasser results. Regarding that most critical of her self-concepts, Dr. Glasser was too young to understand the mission of that acorn seed's grandiosity. She was to "write the greatest book ever written". This book You Matter is that effort.

Has Dr. Glasser even come close to achieving her father's prophesy? You can't lose in the act of informatively answering. What you learn here is important regardless.

From what she calls an inside out perspective, Dr. Glasser in the clearest of terms, teaches mind-body functioning for purposes of your wellness. Your mind is your body. Your body is your mind. They are intertwined. Fitness for life depends on working toward your increasing freedom to enact what you learn here.

Fitness isn't just physical, nutritional, or due to just genetic predisposition nor the conquest of your thoughts through meditation. Here, you've learned about the controlling link to it all, your beliefs. They are your governing 'truths' even if some of those beliefs are false. But the false can be shifted into your current, wholesome, to be enacted truths.

With a Master's in Education and a Doctorate in clinical and educational psychology, Dr. Joyce Glasser shares what you need to know for the wellness of you and through you the survival of our world. Save you as one who matters, guide your children exemplifying the wholesome values of such identity, so that they too believe they matter. By extension and by projection their mattering allows them to save our planet.

Dr. Glasser teaches that every one of us who are enabled to advance their humanity by equally/lovingly/kindly mattering become a united family of humane beings preserving the beauty of both Earth's and humans' nature. Dr. Glasser calls these increasing multitudes of avatars: Earth Angels.

With inspiration from and
In loving memory of her parents
Daniel D. Glasser and Sylvia G. Glasser
With heartfelt gratitude for her brother and sister-in-law
James J. Glasser and Louise R. Glasser
and the blessing to the world of their children:
Daniel R. Glasser
Emily L. Glasser
Mary C. Glasser

OTHER BOOKS by DR. GLASSER

Core Healing: Dissolving the dis-eases of our times. (2007 Heart of the Golden Triangle Publishers. Eustis, FL)

The Elementary School Learning Centers for Independent Study (1971 Parker Publishing Company. West Nyack, NY)

EL CENTRO DE ESTUDIO INDEPENDIENTE EN LAS ESCUELAS PRIMARIAS (1975 Editorial Guadalupe: Buenos Aires, Argentina)

****